PRAISE FOR *BEAN BLOS*

"Infused with considerable charm . . . lyrical, humorous writing . . . a colorful cast of characters, both human and animal, inhabits the book."
—*Kirkus Reviews*

"An engaging account of her family's first year on the farm that will appeal strongly to animal- and nature-lovers." —*Publishers Weekly*

"Warm, humorous, and realistic." —*Library Journal*

"With an incredible eye for detail, Murphey offers insight into the differences in country vs. city living . . . Spending a few hours with Murphey, her family, neighbors, and sixty-three furred and feathered friends is the next best thing to being there." —*Rocky Mountain News*

Sallyann J. Murphey, a former BBC producer, spent more than fifteen years in television production in London, New York, and Chicago before abandoning big cities in 1991. Her first book, *Bean Blossom Dreams: A City Family's Search for a Simple Country Life*, chronicled her family's early experiences on the farm, and was published in 1994. Her second book, *Emma's Christmas Wish*, was published in 1996. She now divides her time between work as an author and as a speaker, lecturing about spiritual ideas. She has appeared on *Oprah*, *Good Morning America*, and National Public Radio. Ms. Murphey lives with her husband, her daughter, and forty-eight assorted animal friends on Bean Blossom Farm in Brown County, Indiana.

BERKLEY BOOKS BY SALLYANN J. MURPHEY

The Zen of Food
Bean Blossom Dreams

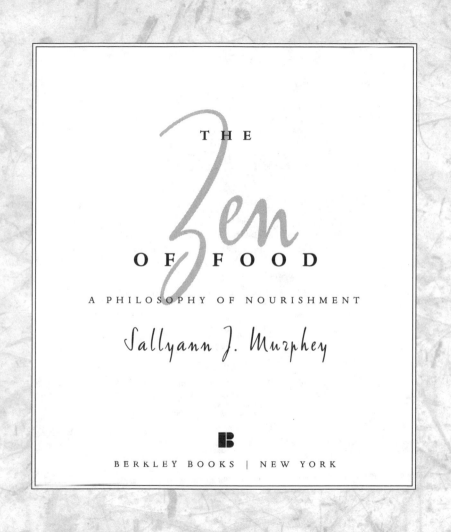

THE

Zen

OF FOOD

A PHILOSOPHY OF NOURISHMENT

Sallyann J. Murphey

BERKLEY BOOKS | NEW YORK

This book is an original publication of The Berkley Publishing Group.

THE ZEN OF FOOD

A Berkley Book / published by arrangement with
the author

PRINTING HISTORY
Berkley trade paperback edition / May 1998

The Penguin Putnam Inc. World Wide Web site address is
http://www.penguinputnam.com

ISBN: 0-425-16311-3

BERKLEY®
Berkley Books are published by The Berkley Publishing Group, a member of
Penguin Putnam Inc.,
200 Madison Avenue, New York, New York 10016.
BERKLEY and the "B" design
are trademarks belonging to Berkley Publishing Corporation.

PRINTED IN THE UNITED STATES OF AMERICA
10   9   8   7   6   5   4   3   2   1

To Greg,
My lover and best friend
And to Charley,
My reason for everything

Contents

CONTENTS

THE

OF FOOD

On the Menu Today . . .

BOUT FIFTY THOUSAND WORDS," MY EDITOR
said. "Not a recipe book—just a collection of your
thoughts about food . . . Would you be interested?"
What author in their right mind would say no? "Of course!" I
replied—with more enthusiasm than I felt at the time. My re-
flections about food were pretty straightforward: I love to grow
it; I love to cook it; I love to eat it and I can think of nothing better to share with my family and friends—only 49,971 words to
go. But then I started to think. Food is, after all, one of our main
preoccupations from the moment we're born. We spend the first

months in life communicating lustily about little else: "Feed me, I need to live. Feed me, I need to grow. Feed me now, now, NOW!!!" Our instinct to eat is so closely entwined with our instinct to survive that it's impossible to separate the two. What drives the human baby today drove humankind in its infancy to stand upright, stretching for the fruit on the tree, reaching to see above the tall grasses and spot the grazing herds. Following these herds brought us out of Africa and scattered us to the four corners of the earth, where we discovered and adapted indigenous plants and animals into an almost infinite variety of regional cuisines. We've been experimenting ever since—the only species on the planet to prepare its meals. Dinner has been elevated into an art form and has become an essential part of our rituals, our religions, our very self-esteem. What we eat as individuals reveals volumes about us—from our educational background to our economic status. What a society eats tells the world about its history, its geography, its political system and cultural priorities. The availability of crops out of season and exotic imports are benchmarks of sophistication, while abuses of food are usually symptoms of much deeper ills. The bulimic and anorexic are both rooted in a distorted image of ourselves, while many of the obese use food in a desperate attempt to fill some other inner void.

In America, we are of two minds about the subject. On one hand, we find it fascinating enough to have bought forty million cookbooks last year; on the other, we are happy to reduce the entire business to patty-shaped fuel, to be eaten in our laps on our way to more "important" things. Part of us delights in the quality and abundant variety of dishes available today, while the other part, the Puritan ancestor in us, latches onto every pseudo-scientific reason to deny ourselves the pleasure. Food is constantly getting the blame for heart disease, high-blood pressure, even some forms of cancer, yet we bemoan the loss of home-cooked meals, when the American family gathered around the table and spent time getting to know each other over Mom's gloriously high-fat dishes. Today, our two-income parents no longer have the energy to make elaborate dinners, yet cooking schools are doing brisk business all around the country. This paradox is symbolic of one of the great issues of the 1990s: our search for balance, the reexamination of our priorities, the struggle in an ever-more pressured world for real meaning in our lives.

Suddenly fifty thousand words doesn't seem nearly enough for all there is to say and I must remind myself of my brief: a *small* collection of *personal* thoughts about "the Zen of food." *Chambers Twentieth Century Dictionary* defines the word *Zen* as "a

Japanese Buddhist sect which holds that the truth is not in scriptures, but in man's own heart if he will but strive to find it by meditation and self-mastery." However, anyone born after 1950 knows that this noun has now evolved into an adjective. Today, something is *zen* if it frees the mind from life's daily stresses and allows it to contemplate the world in a detached way. The sensation is, by implication, pleasant and relaxing—a sort of sauna for the soul. A zen experience should leave us refreshed, with a new perspective on whatever it was we were thinking about. In this case, the topic is food and this book will journey through some of its pleasures, its meanings, and its history, in the hope that the writer and reader alike may discover fresh passion and respect for a subject that must concern us all, to a lesser or greater extent, every day of our lives.

S.J.M.

The X Factor

WHAT QUALITIES MAKE A GOOD COOK? MY HUS-band (one of the best cooks I know) and I were debating this over breakfast, just the other day. The question had been prompted by the feast that Greg had laid before us: golden clouds of scrambled eggs, sitting on rafts of nutty seven-grain toast and flanked by perfectly crisped bacon; followed by blueberry pancakes, plump with *real* fruit and drizzled in a beautifully balanced mixture of melted butter and maple syrup. The meal was delicious, both as a whole and in each of its separate elements, and it made me wonder how it was that another cook could have taken exactly the same ingredients and produced a totally different result. What is it about Greg's cooking that lifts it from the skilled to the sublime?

The ability to follow a recipe, we decided, was irrelevant. For one thing, most good cooks never do. They like to judge things by sight, taste, and smell, adding a splash of this and pinch of that—artists building up their canvas. Recipes should be only rough guides (with the exception of baking, which is a different discipline) and to follow one exactly is a bit like painting by numbers—strictly for the beginner.

Understanding one's ingredients is, however, essential. If cooks don't know that a fresh egg yolk should sit like a deep yellow dome on an island of stiff white, or that bacon must be fried over a moderate heat, they have no business making breakfast. And if they don't appreciate the delicate alchemy of cream, butter, and eggs that is the difference between a cloud of scrambled eggs and a smashed-up omelette, they are not ready for the more complex wizardry of soups, sauces, and stews. Good cooks can conjure up the tastes of ingredients in their minds and can "previsualize" the effect of one upon the other before they've even turned on the stove. Great chefs carry whole databases of food in their heads and can arrange blind dates between unlikely partners that turn into happy and mutually enhancing marriages. It took a great chef to introduce raspberries to chocolate, duck to orange, or even baked Brie to gooseberry sauce—and this inventiveness is part of what we look for when we pay vast amounts to eat at a great chef's restaurant. We also expect their raw materials to be the best: the freshest vegetables, the most succulent meats, seasonings that come from a real plant and not the dried-up shavings from some bottle on a shelf. These ingredients should then be put together into dishes which are as pleasing to the eye as they are to the tongue and served in a setting that is equally alluring.

Yet even when all these elements are in place, we don't always enjoy a great meal. We come away feeling that the dinner was delicious more in theory than in fact and that, despite the seeming perfection of it all, it lacked a certain depth—dinner was missing something. This Factor X, I believe, is the subtle quality that makes food truly memorable. When it is present, the simplest dish tastes special; when it is not, the most skillfully prepared meal somehow fails to please.

My first acquaintance with Factor X was made one January night in London while I was still a child. I had taken the subway home from school to find, on emerging from the bowels of the

earth, that I had traveled into a storm. The rain was tumbling out
of the sky. It bounced off the pavement, flinging itself sideways
under helpless umbrellas, pounding at the halogen streetlights,
which hissed and spat out their disgruntled response. I stared
gloomily at the downpour from the smelly safety of the subway
station, wondering whether to walk the twelve blocks home in
what my school laughingly called a raincoat, or risk my mother's
wrath by waiting it out. No contest. I pulled up my collar and
trudged into the bone-chilling British night. . . .

Forty-five minutes later my mother opened the door to a blue-
tinged twelve-year-old, dripping puddles over the lobby floor. She
gave a little shriek and pulled me inside, marching me straight off
to the bathroom. Taps were turned, clothes were stripped, and
towels set on the rack to warm. "Get in!" she ordered, before dis-
appearing in the direction of the kitchen. By the time she re-
turned, I was neck-deep in jasmine-scented water, beginning to
feel more human again. "Drink this!" she said, shoving a large
mug between my defrosting hands. It was hot chocolate—not
the thin, powdery kind but the real thing, made with pieces of
chocolate and butter, melted into creamy milk. I took a sip and
felt a sense of well-being spread right down to my toes. Both
body and soul flushed with pleasure—not only at its warmth and

sweetness, but also at the spirit with which it had been made. Mum had been ill for some time and too busy on inward survival to focus much on the outside. This simple thing, this common cup of cocoa, was a declaration of love—of her care for me—and, as such, was the most delicious drink I'd ever tasted.

When I grew up and acquired a kitchen of my own, I learned that the success of a meal was actually a two-way street that depended not only on the spirit with which it was offered, but also on the manner in which it was received. A good cook is an unselfish host, who anticipates the tastes, the expectations, even the comfort level of his or her guests. Over the years I've made beef Wellington for confirmed vegetarians, bouillabaisse for a friend who's allergic to fish, and the most spectacular orange creme caramel for a visitor who was forbidden to eat eggs. Now I've learned to ask about my guests' likes and dislikes, food allergies, diets, etc., *before* they come to dinner!

I've also learned that menus must be tailored to fit the occasion. On the wrong day, a six-course meal served on one's best bone china can overwhelm, reducing conversation to churchlike whispers as guests struggle with the attendant silverware and crystal. The balance of the evening is destroyed because the focus is on the food, rather than on the people eating it. Most get-togethers call for more casual fare, a dinner that can be enjoyed comfortably, while still being a challenge to the cook. Spaghetti Bolognese, garlic bread, and salad become haute cuisine when the bread is homemade; the salad a combination of avocados, red leaf lettuce, and a fluffy mustard mayonnaise; and the sauce is a lovingly prepared mixture of shredded sirloin and pork, finely chopped onions, carrots, tomatoes, and garlic, a touch of cinnamon, brown sugar, and nutmeg, all left to simmer gently for hours with regular additions of rough red wine. Add to this fruit, cheese, and a tangy *tarte aux citrons,* and you have a meal that a great chef would not be ashamed of.

You should also have some very happy guests—although there are still no guarantees. This is where Factor X becomes the responsibility of the consumers rather than the cook. It is their job to appreciate the food—not with words necessarily but with their senses. A meal can only be memorable if its participants have truly seen, smelled, and tasted all the subtleties of it. I lost count of the number of disappointing evenings I spent in my twenties watching my efforts being shoveled down like dog meat, or pushed around the plate while the perpetrator concentrated on the brilliance of his own repartee. One young man even asked for ketchup to go with a salmon that had been baked in fresh tarragon and lime: I almost despaired. I was beginning to believe that the love of food belonged to a past age, when people still moved slowly enough to savor their stew, until another stormy night in January, while I was living in Manhattan.

I'd been out on a date—not the usual boring horror but a meeting of two minds, a wonderful evening that I wished would never end. As we arrived back at my apartment the heavens opened, so I broke the unwritten rule and invited him in. "Coffee, tea, hot chocolate?" I offered.

"Hot chocolate . . ." he replied. I only had the powder, but I made it up with milk and a touch of orange essence, topped off with floated cream and a twist of orange peel. My escort took a sip, looked serious for a second, then announced that it was "delicious." It was the moment, as we admitted to each other later, when Greg and I both knew that one day we would wed.

Snowed In

OW, ELEVEN YEARS LATER, WE LIVE ON A FARM in southern Indiana with our nine-year-old daughter, Charley, and forty-eight assorted furred and feathered friends. With hindsight, you could say that food was one of the main reasons we moved here. Our souls could no longer survive the endless stream of plastic meals delivered to our door after twelve-hour working days. We wanted the time to cook our own food and the space in which grow it. We wanted our then-baby to understand the connection between the chicken and the egg, the apple and the tree. We wanted her to appreciate the miracle on her plate and the work, skill, and love that had gone into putting it there. We couldn't bear the idea of mealtimes being little more than pit stops to refuel. Food isn't simply nourishment, it has become our symbol for the nurturing we should all receive. Moving to the country may seem a bit extreme, but we knew that it was the only way we would abandon the fast track and achieve some balance in our lives.

We may have got more than we bargained for. Food here isn't just a symbol or a pleasure, it's an imperative, a constant concern that defines each season. Even in the depths of winter, we cannot get away from it. A six-inch snowfall will cut us off from the world and fling us into a seemingly endless cycle of feeding the animals, feeding the fire, feeding ourselves so that we'll have the energy to feed the animals and feed the fire again. The bitter cold reduces every life on the farm to its basic priorities: shelter, warmth, and the consumption of food.

I see it when I struggle out to water the horses, moving from one cozy pocket of shelter (the house) to another (the barn), passing smaller homes in hedges and trees along the way. Everyone is grateful simply to be out of the howling wind, with relatively full stomachs. The barn animals eat voraciously, fueling their central heating systems, nature driving them to stock up when they can. The rest of the time they sleep, conserving every drop of energy for the important task of keeping warm. Even the wild creatures aren't stirring. The snow remains virgin, free of the lines of tracks that will crisscross it as soon as the storm has passed. I picture foxes and raccoons curled up in their burrows, in a state of suspended animation. The only movements on the landscape are flashes of color from the songbirds as they fly in frantic relay from nests to feeders, the one source of sustenance in their frozen world.

Back at the house, Greg is making pot roast. The smell of onions softening in butter has already combined with the faint fragrance from the broth I made the night before. This is dense food that reminds me of the great logs of oak we put into the stove once the blaze is going. Oak doesn't flame up quickly like the sassafras and locust that start the fire off: it burns hot and red, releasing its warmth steadily for hours. Pot roast is the same, satisfying us in a deeper way than quick meals ever can.

We expect things too fast these days. Speed has become synonymous with efficiency and efficiency is automatically good. We reflect our technological age, forgetting that what is desirable in computers, accountants, and planes can actually stunt the creative process. In general, great art and good cooking both require time. There is no comparison, for instance, between the chicken stock that has been boiled into existence over a couple of hours and the rich broth that is lovingly coaxed to life in a large pot on a low flame, usually overnight. The first is pale yellow water, vaguely reminiscent of fowl, while the second is a dark gold treasure, mined from bones that have gone soft in the effort to yield up their last drop of flavor. The preparation work for the cook is exactly the same; the rest is a matter of patience. Like the wild creatures around us, staying still sometimes achieves the most.

This can also apply to simple foods—as we discover each time our power goes out. In storms like these, ice gathers on the lines, eventually tearing them down. We have become old hands at surviving without electricity, often for many hours. It is not something to be feared anymore, it is something to be enjoyed, a brief interlude when life moves to a different rhythm, when we can feel our powers of perception sharpen as our heartbeats calm. We read, we talk, we light the kerosene lamps and cook on the woodstove—a slow procedure that seems to bring out the best in everything. Soups taste soupier, toast is toastier, and pots of tea produce the deep, rich drink that I remember from my childhood. Part of this may be seasoned by pride in our independence, by the joy we feel at surviving off the grid; but even the urban cook needs a profound respect for time.

It certainly pays off as far as Greg's pot roast is concerned. When darkness falls, he produces shining plates of it, awash in silky gravy. The meat falls off the bone, its beefiness concentrated into every bite. It is food that warms, food that fuels, food that binds us together as a family in the amber glow of the oil lamps. It is why we came. . . .

Greg's Yankee Pot Roast

beef pot roast	soup bones
onions	4 sticks of celery
1 green pepper	4 carrots
2 cups of beef broth	1 16-ounce can of tomatoes
(homemade or canned)	1 small bunch parsley
2 bay leaves	seasoned pepper
Seasoned salt	fresh ground black pepper
Kitchen Bouquet	2 cloves of garlic

½ cup red wine

1 cup chopped mushrooms

½ stick butter

2 teaspoons flour

1. Preheat oven to 350 degrees. 2. Finely chop onions and crush the garlic cloves. 3. Melt the butter in an ovenproof casserole. 4. Brown onions and garlic in the melted butter. 5. Season the pot roast with the salt and peppers and add to casserole dish. 6. Brown meat. 7. Add the soup bones, beef broth, tomatoes, wine, bay leaves, and 1 capful of Kitchen Bouquet. 8. Cover the casserole and put in the oven, where it should bake for at least 3 hours. 9. Roughly chop the carrots, celery, and green pepper. 10. Add at 2 hours. 11. Wash the mushrooms thoroughly and chop. 12. Add in the final hour's cooking. 13. At the end of 3 hours, take the meat, bones, and bay leaves out. 14. Thicken the vegetable gravy with the flour mixed in a little hot water. 15. Add a few splashes of Kitchen Bouquet for color. 16. Serve the slices of the meat, topped with the gravy and vegetables on a bed of wide egg noodles.

On the Road to Ostia

INALLY, THE SNOW PLOW SHOWS UP, THE WEATHER warms, and it's back to work for all of us—or at least it is for Greg and Charley. I write at home, so my work never really ends; it is just put on hold while the family's around. When they are not, I plunge in, reluctant to stop even to eat. The hours fly by and food only comes to mind when my body starts sending out a gurgling SOS. Lunch is almost always a plate of salami, cheeses, and fruit, eaten with a hunk of good bread. I don't get bored because there are wide varieties of each ingredient, which, when put together, remind me of picnics, lazy summers, and one of my life's most memorable meals.

It happened on a vacation to Italy that was full of golden moments: the dinner we had by the Canale Della Giudecca in Venice, when we feasted on *canoce* and *caparozzoli* (mantis shrimp and clams); our lunch in Bologna La Grassa (Bologna the Fat), where we lingered over the best lasagna Bolognese we'd ever tasted, washed down with chilled glasses of that region's jealously guarded wine, a delightfully dry cousin to the more usual sweet sparkling red Lambrusco; and then there was that *zuppa di mare* we cooked for ourselves with the sackful of succulent mussels we'd harvested while snorkeling at the base of Mount Circeo—once home, they say, to the legendary sorceress, Circe. They are experiences I will never forget, but one outweighs them all: our picnic on the road to Ostia.

We had spent the night before in a little village in the Umbrian mountains, where the spotlessly clean rooms were four dollars each and where locals had gathered in the taverna to listen to us speak English! The next morning, we wanted to buy a snack to keep us going on the road, so I ran over to the village grocery and stepped into another century. The little shop was a treasure trove of food. Hams, sausage, and salamis were strung from the ceiling, struggling for space with straw-covered casks of wine. On the floor, boxes of peaches still damp with orchard dew competed with barrels of black olives, sacks of beans, and shelves laden with wheels of Pecorino cheese. The baked goods of the day were on the counter at the back—round loaves of floury bread and little bags of *brutti ma buoni* (ugly but good) sugar and almond cookies. The store was fragrant with the smells of ground coffee, spices, and the fresh sawdust on the floor. I didn't know where to begin and told the owner so, who laughed and produced a small paring knife. He moved slowly among his riches, explaining where each had come from and how it had been made, while he cut a slice of this and a snicket of that for his student to sample. Finally, I chose what I wanted and my host wrapped it all up. The entire bill was about twelve dollars, which mollified my friend, who had been waiting impatiently outside.

We didn't open the little paper packages until that afternoon, when we had maneuvered around Rome and found our way to Ostia. Here, on the crumbling walls of the port the Romans began building in the fourth century B.C., we spread our tablecloth and set up lunch. It was a beautiful day. A warm breeze was blowing off the Mediterranean, sharpening our appetites and making the solemn cypress trees dance and quiver in the sunlight. Italian sunshine enriches everything it touches. It saturates colors, turning blue, yellow, and red into cyan, ocher, and vermilion—the colors we see repeated in so many of this country's paintings. We couldn't have asked for a prettier setting—not that our food needed any help.

If I close my eyes I can still taste it all: the sweetness of the Gorgonzola, young enough to spread creamily across our chunks of bread; the bread itself, golden and crusty on the outside, with a chewy pale gray dough inside that tasted almost prebuttered; the wine, a hearty Chianti Classico, stamped with the black cockerel that proved it did indeed come from the vineyards between Florence and Siena and wasn't the washed-out version we so often buy abroad; the salami, a rich spicy confection made by the store owner's brother-in-law, who prided himself on raising the best pork in the region. We wouldn't have argued with him; this was unlike any we had tasted before, full of layers of flavor— garlic, salt, black pepper, the meat itself—all blended together in a mix that stood our taste buds on end and immediately satisfied our stomachs. The peaches were an ideal complement to it; lush and fragrant, they burst on our tongues and cleansed our palates with sweet juice.

How often, I wondered, had these ancient walls witnessed a

meal like this? Had some Roman citizen sat on these bone-colored blocks two thousand years ago and eaten something similar? It was quite possible. The Romans liked to save their main meal (their *cena*) for the evening. At midday, they preferred to eat light—bread, cheese, olives—or a snack from one of the many street vendors, possibly a *piada,* a piece of flattened dough topped with pickled fish and onions that was the ancestor of the pizza. A Roman would have understood our lunch, it would have been familiar. We were enjoying food that was utterly in synch with its surroundings.

In the years since, I have often tried to re-create that picnic. I've scoured delicatessens for salamis and cheeses, and spent hours baking a variety of breads—but they are all pale echoes of the past. Perhaps a memorable meal is only meant to be eaten once. Perhaps its unique tastes and circumstances should remain just that, a gift from Providence to be cherished and stored away until some gray winter's day, when it can be brought out again to flood the dining room with sunlight.

By Bread Alone

OST ITALIAN RECIPES ASIDE, VERY LITTLE IN the kitchen is more zen than the act of baking bread. There's something uniquely fulfilling about it: the fragrance of warm yeast; the magic of the dough doubling in size; the feeling of achievement when the loaves sit cooling on the rack; and the delight in tasting them fresh from the oven. Home-baked bread is one of life's multilayered blessings and I can't understand why more people don't make their own.

Our friends offer the usual excuses. They're too busy, it's too hard and anyway, they've got that nice little bakery just down the block. These are stressed-out people who feel compelled to use each minute to its maximum advantage. The idea that they might derive any benefit from a morning's baking is almost subversive, a kooky claim that belongs to the world of earth mothers and New Agers. Since I am neither, I would like to invite them—and all skeptics—into my kitchen now, to watch me make a simple loaf of bread. . . .

I put the oven on before I began writing, so the room is suitably muggy. Let's start by getting the ingredients together. I'm going to make one of the Murphey family's favorites, a *pain d'ail,* quite literally a garlic bread, but one that has all its creamy garlic butter already mixed into the dough. The recipe comes from my baking bible, *The Complete Book of Breads* by Bernard Clayton, and calls for six cloves of garlic, softened sweet butter, bread flour, yeast, salt, sugar, dry milk, and water.

I should also set out the equipment. One of the secrets to making any kind of cooking a zen experience is to get organized before you begin. There's nothing worse than finding, halfway through a wonderful creation, that someone's sprouting seed in the bread pan, or that the essential ingredient has vanished from the fridge. I prefer to deal with bad news when there's still time to do something about it. Today I need two medium loaf pans, a garlic press, my marble board, a small bowl for the butter, a clean cloth, and a large mixing bowl. It took me years to find a bread bowl that I liked. They usually don't make them big enough these days, and when they do, they're aluminum (too light) or plastic (too absorbent). The few pottery bowls I'd seen were more decorative than utilitarian and priced accordingly. Then one Sunday afternoon, I was browsing around a little country store and there it was—a humongous, steep-sided earthenware bowl, roughly glazed in dark blue. It weighs a good ten pounds, but it doesn't slip around and it's large enough to hold vast amounts of dough.

Now we can get started. First, the garlic cloves must be blanched in an inch of boiling water for a minute, then run under the cold tap. The cloves are fresh and crisp, without a hint of green shoots or overdry, papery skin. (I'm not against the pre-prepared varieties, they're very useful as a background flavor, but when you actually want the taste of garlic, nothing can substitute for the real thing.) I'll put the cloves through a press, then mix them with the softened butter. Hmm . . . that delicious smell is just a mild hint of what's to come. Let's set this aside and move over to the mixing bowl.

At this point bread making becomes magical. Look at these

simple ingredients—flour, salt, sugar, yeast, and dried milk. Who would predict that they could amount to anything more than a bland mush? Yet add hot water, stir with a wooden spoon, and we have the beginnings of a small miracle. This is when I blend in the butter and the scents of yeast and garlic become deliciously strong. I wish I'd eaten something before I began because the smell is making me ravenously hungry. As it drifts through the house Charley and Greg always appear in the kitchen, unconsciously driven to search for a snack. Here comes Greg now, rummaging through the kitchen cupboards. If he's true to form, he'll be hovering over my shoulder in a second, barking at the bowl. I've told him before that this doesn't speed up the baking process, but it seems to make him feel better. . . .

I have to turn the batter into a dough, so I'm going to add more flour . . . a little more. . . . There, it's solid enough to pick up—which means that it's ready to knead.

Kneading brings the bread to life. It makes the gluten in the flour form an elastic honeycomb into which the yeast will puff little bubbles of CO_2 while the bread is baking. It is also the most zen part of this zen endeavor. There should be a rhythm to it: slap the dough onto the board, push it down with the heel of the hand, fold it over, push it, pick it up, and slap it down again. It's a mesmerizing exercise, an ancient dance that spins back through time, linking us to all the others who have kneaded bread before. Slap, push, fold, push . . . like our pioneer foremothers, many of whom baked upward of a thousand loaves a year. Slap, push, fold, push . . . like the medieval bakers at English manor houses who made the round flat bread, known as a trencher, that lined the lords' and ladies' wooden plates. (These were always shared, one trencher to two companions, from the Latin cum, meaning "with," and panis, meaning "bread.") Slap, push, fold, push . . . like the household slaves of the Roman empire, who baked the delicately petaled loaves that were found petrified at Pompeii. Slap, push, fold, push . . . like the ancient Egyptians who, historians say, discovered leavened bread by accident, then had the courage to eat it and the creativity to make it rise again.

As I work, the dough metamorphoses beneath my fingers— from sticky, cloying goo to a smooth, velvet mound. When it looks and feels as firm as a baby's bottom, it is fully kneaded and can be set in a warm place to double in size. The first stage is finished: it took all of twenty-five minutes. We can now go and do something else for an hour, because the dough has become a living thing that will grow without our supervision.

This process never ceases to amaze me. What a gift to humankind—a food quite literally from the heavens. Is it any wonder that the "staff of life" has been sanctified by so many religions? "Give us this day our daily bread" is a prayer for more than just a meal. It is a prayer for security, for the ability to feed ourselves even in the most extreme conditions. Alaskan frontiersmen prized bread so much that crocks of sourdough starter were valued legacies willed to the next generation. A landscape may be a barren wilderness, but where there's bread, there is life.

It's hard not to peek, but that would spoil the surprise when I lift the cloth off the bowl and find a white cloud inside. Sometimes I'm tempted to leave it and see how large it will get, but the dough wouldn't thank me. It would develop a bad attack of gas and take its revenge by becoming coarse bread that tastes like stale beer. So I must end its labors by turning it back onto the board and "punching it down." The escaping air sounds like a hiss of relief. A couple more minutes' kneading and it's ready to be divided between the two pans. When it has risen an inch above the pan rims, it will be time to bake.

And that's about it. For a total of forty minutes' work I have two golden loaves, a husband with the happiest of smiles on his face, and the deep satisfaction of knowing that I can feed my family, even in hard times. It is as if an ancient contract with the four elements has been renewed, in which they promise to sustain us—provided that we're willing, on occasion, to take our survival into our own hands.

Pain D'Ail (from Bernard Clayton's Complete Book of Breads)

This recipe makes two medium-sized loaves, which—wrapped well—freeze beautifully and will keep without any noticeable loss of flavor for about six months. This bread is particularly delicious lightly toasted and spread with a garlic-and-herb cream cheese. My thanks again to Mr. Clayton for allowing me to reproduce it here:

*4 to 6 garlic cloves,
peeled (depending on
strength desired)
¼ cup (½ stick butter),
room temperature*

*1 package dry yeast
2 teaspoons salt
1 tablespoon sugar
⅓ cup nonfat dry milk*

5 to 5½ cups bread or
all-purpose flour,
approximately

2¼ cups hot water
(120–130 degrees)

Baking pans: 2 medium (8X4-inch) baking pans, greased or Teflon.

1. In a saucepan blanch the garlic cloves in boiling water for 1 minute. 2. Remove and place under cold running water for a few moments. 3. Pound into a smooth paste in a mortar or put through a garlic press. 4. Soften the butter and mix with the garlic. 5. Set to one side.

Mr. Clayton then divides his instructions into two methods—one using a food processor and one made by hand or mixer.

By hand or mixer

1. Measure 3 cups flour into a mixer or mixing bowl. 2. Add the yeast, salt, sugar, and dry milk. Stir to blend. 3. If by hand, pour the water into the flour and stir vigorously with a wooden spoon to blend thoroughly. 4. Drop in the garlic butter and mix it into the batter. 5. Add flour, 1/4 cup at a time, to develop shaggy, rough dough that can be lifted to the work surface to knead. 6. If by mixer, attach flat beater. 7. With the mixer running, pour in the water to form a thick batter. 8. Drop in the garlic butter and

mix for 2 minutes at medium speed. 9. Add flour, 1/4 cup at a time. 10. When the dough clings to the flat beater without mixing, attach the dough hook, adding more flour if necessary to form a soft ball around the revolving hook.

Kneading
1. If by hand, place the dough on the floured work surface and knead with a push-turn-fold motion to create a dough that is soft and elastic. Add sprinkles of flour if sticky. 2. If under the mixer dough hook, continue with the machine running. If the dough should cling to the sides of the bowl, add light sprinkles of flour. The dough will form a soft ball around the revolving arm. Knead for 10 minutes by hand or in the mixer.

By processor
1. Prepare the garlic butter, as above, and set aside. 2. Attach the short plastic dough blade. 3. Measure 4 cups flour into the work bowl and add the yeast, salt, sugar, and dry milk. Pulse to blend. 4. With the machine running, pour the water through the feed tube to form a heavy batter. 5. Drop in the garlic butter and process for a few seconds to blend. 6. Uncover the work bowl and 1/2 cup flour. At the same time with a rubber spatula loosen

and push to the center any dry ingredients stuck along the outer
edges of the bowl. 7. With the machine running add the flour
through the feed tube, 1/4 cup at a time, to form a mass that will
spin with the blade and clean the sides of the bowl. 8. Knead with
the processor running for about 1 1/2 minutes. The dough
should be slightly sticky and very elastic when kneading is complete. Pull and stretch the dough between your hands to test its
consistency; if necessary, return the dough to the work bowl to
process for a few seconds more.

First rising
Place the dough in a greased bowl, cover tightly with plastic
wrap, and put aside to double in volume, about 1 hour. (If prepared with a new fast-rising yeast and at the recommended
higher temperatures, reduce the rising times by about half.)

Shaping
1. Turn the dough onto the work surface, knead briefly to push
out the air bubbles, and divide in half. 2. Press each half into a flat
oval, about the length of the pan. Fold in half lengthwise, pinch
the seam together, tuck in the ends, and drop seam down into the
baking pan.

Second rising

1. Cover the pans with parchment or wax paper and let rise until the dough has doubled in volume, about 1 inch above the pan rim, 45 minutes. 2. Preheat the oven to 375 degrees 20 minutes before baking.

Baking

1. Place the baking pans on the middle shelf of the oven. 2. The loaves will be a light brown when baked, about 40 minutes. 3. To test for doneness, turn one loaf out of its pan and thump the bottom crust. If it sounds hard and hollow, the bread is done. If not, return to the oven for an additional 10 minutes, without the tin. (If using a convection oven, reduce heat 50 degrees.) 4. Turn the loaves from the pans onto a rack to cool.

$$\mathcal{S}eeds\ldots$$

EBRUARY IS A MISERABLE MONTH: EVEN THE calendar tries to get it over quickly. It's the dregs of winter, when wood fires lose their romance and heavy meals no longer appeal. We are desperate for spring and only kept sane by the signs of our inevitable march toward it: later sunsets, the first warm breeze, Valentine's Day, the return of robins, wild garlic sprouting in the grass—all promises that the ordeal is almost over. Our attention starts to swing outside to the muddy cesspool at the back that was once our vegetable garden. We get through February by planning the delights that will grow there in the warmer months to come.

Some choices have already been made: seeds from the best of last year's cucumbers, green beans, peppers, and corn—along with Greg's twenty-eight favorite types of tomato—were saved last fall and are sleeping peacefully at the back of the refrigerator. While others come from those gloriously seductive catalogs and will be wild adventures for the year, romantic names to be measured against the reality of our heavy clay soil and scorching August heat: Rainbow Inca corn and Sweet Dumpling squash, Shungiku chrysanthemum greens and the charming "Bubbles" brussels sprout. Not all of them will make it, but for now their seeds sit in shining piles on the kitchen table, pregnant with possibilities.

A seed is an extraordinary thing—a tiny package of life that can lie inert for years, until it is given just the right amount of moisture, light, and heat. Then it will burst forth, revealing a plant that may have once built empires or brought the ancient world to the brink of war. Seeds have shaped our destiny ever since Pleistocene man first planted "emmer" and "einkorn" (wild strains of wheat), twelve thousand years ago. Stable communities formed around those fields, bringing with them the notion of property boundaries, ownership, and the accumulation of wealth. The great civilizations of Samaria, Egypt, Greece, and Rome were partly founded on their ability to produce, store, sell, and trade an overabundance of grain. The Romans prized wheat so much that they preserved the granaries when they razed the rest of Carthage to the ground. Grain was a form of currency, a tool of power, it even defined your social class: the finer the flour, the better the bread, the richer you were likely to be.

In later centuries another seed rose to the status of a national treasure: *piper nigrum,* black pepper (actually a dried berry), was so valued that it was given routinely to powerful men as a bribe. Emperor Theodosius III sent some to Attila the Hun, and the Visigoths demanded that part of their tribute be paid in peppercorns when they marched into Rome. Pepper drove Marco Polo (a spice merchant) east and that other Italian, Christopher Columbus, west in search of an easier spice route. Columbus didn't find one, of course, but what he did bring back were seeds that would change the world.

Imagine, for a moment, the Germans or Irish without potatoes, or Italian cooking tomato-free. Imagine a diet without corn, beans, chocolate, chili peppers, pineapple, or peanuts, and you begin to see the major contribution that foods from this hemisphere have made. At first, the Europeans were suspicious, unwilling to abandon their established farming ways, but gradually—as the poor discovered that potatoes or corn could feed many more per acre—the crops began to spread. By the eighteenth century, potatoes underpinned a population explosion in Northern Europe that would usher in the Industrial Revolution and—as the cities grew—potatoes fed the new workforces flocking to the factories. In Southern Europe, corn (or maize, as they call it) performed much the same role, sustaining such increases in population among the poor that the Greeks, Serbs, and Vlachs were able, eventually, to form the armies that overthrew their Turkish overlords.

The European love of food springs partly from a recognition of its power. The effects of feast and famine are imprinted on their genetic memory, driving even young cooks today into making the most of what they have. Nothing goes to waste and the simplest crop is reinvented again and again in a wide variety of delicious dishes. No one messes with mealtimes (as executives in the French air industry discovered recently, when they tried and failed to curtail their workers' lunch break), because meals are sacrosanct occasions when whole families affirm their prosperity through food.

Many modern-day Americans don't feel the same. This is a land of plenty where the people have become accustomed to the abundance on their plates. We don't make the best of berries in the summer or fresh vegetables in the fall, because we can buy them at supermarkets throughout the seasons. This seemingly limitless supply has made us profligate, preferring to throw away more food than India eats in a year than recycle our leftovers into another meal. The chain has been broken. We have lost our natural respect for the fragile journey of seed, to plant, to precious harvest—and we are the poorer for it. Our culture suffers because many of the old family recipes are being forgotten, while newer ones are not being invented to take their place. America's cuisine depends increasingly on what is being created in its restaurants, which means that our families suffer, too—cut loose from the anchors of tradition and a daily communion around the dinner table. This adds to modern society's feeling of rootlessness, robbing us of both a sense of history and context, and of hope for a future where we can pass our culture on. Above all, our spirits are the losers. In removing ourselves from the cycle of life, we give up our power over it, leaving ourselves vulnerable and insecure—knowing in our heart of hearts that, were famine to strike tomorrow, we would be less equipped to protect ourselves than prehistoric man.

These are some of the reasons why Greg and I plant seeds. When we lived in the city, they gave each year rhythm and connected us to a deeper reality than we found around us at the time. Since we've moved down here, seeds have taught us that a good harvest is a gift—not a given—demanding patience, hard work, and the humility to know that we are part of nature and not here to impose our will upon her. The skills and satisfactions of growing our own food are among the greatest legacies we will leave our child, who will be able to sustain herself—whatever life may bring. That thought gives us a sense of pride, a feeling of confidence in the future, a dream to chase away our February blues.

Good Food 101

WANT TO GO HOME NOW." TWO BIG BLUE EYES
stared at me defiantly. It was supposed to be a
treat—a trip to the Children's Museum for Charley
and her friend, followed by dinner at the Greek Isles, my daughter's then-favorite restaurant. Charley liked everything about the
place: the pitta bread, the keftethakia (little meat balls), the shimmering belly dancer who performed three times a night, but
most of all she loved shouting "Opahh!" as the flames leaped
from the *tsaganaki*, before she plunged into platefuls of this bubbling cheese. Her friend, Suzie, clearly didn't agree. She poked

suspiciously at each dish, refusing to touch a thing, with a thin-lipped expression that read "this just ain't fittin'." As I watched her I wondered where our love affair with food begins. I had thought it was a passion that grew with age, but the stubborn little face in front of me suggested otherwise. This five-year-old's mind had already snapped shut and Suzie was probably condemned to a lifetime of pizza and bologna sandwiches.

Children are conservative little creatures, who like that which they're most used to. Their taste buds begin as soft clay, which is molded, initially, by their parents' habits. Thus a Sri Lankan toddler will tuck into curry that would bring tears to a Westerner's eyes, or a Chinese baby can cheerfully survive on endless bowls of rice. Eating for satisfaction rather than survival is a learned behavior, and both Greg and I will be forever grateful to our families for the lessons they taught us.

Many of my happiest childhood memories revolve around food. In the early days meals meant comfort, nurture, a feeling of safety. Sunny breakfasts of soft-boiled eggs and buttered toast; Victoria sponge cake, or baked rice pudding in front of the nursery fire—simple fare made special by my mother's clever hand. She was a wonderful cook who couldn't resist dabbling with the humblest dishes. Her rice pudding was creamy perfection, cooked with a hint of nutmeg and served with a large, fruity spoonful of strawberry jam; her cakes were light as air; even the toast was buttered edge to edge and cut into convenient strips. It was the fifties then and women were more domestic, but Mum was no June Cleaver. She was an actress, a dark beauty with a temperament that betrayed her Irish-Spanish ancestry. When I was small, she was working hard in a weekly TV drama series. Her meals were offered as gifts, proof to us (and to her) that she was still paying attention.

She learned this trick from her mother, my grandmother, who also expressed herself through food. Nana Moyce, as I knew her, was a tiny Victorian with a strong jaw, who had fought her way through dental school in an age when "nice" women didn't work. She was, as the British say, as tough as old boots—until it came to her cooking. Her steak pies were the loving words she rarely spoke and her mouthwatering desserts were her caresses. Every Saturday, I would sit in the old kitchen, still decorated in the creams and pale greens of the thirties, and watch her make our lunch. "Idle hands . . ." she'd warn, letting me stitch dolls' pillows on her ancient black-and-gold sewing machine while she rattled pans, peeled vegetables, and made the sauce for her spectacular syrup pudding.

Golden-syrup pudding is a classic British dish that combines two of our favorite things: golden syrup—a syrup made from cane sugar that tastes like liquid toffee—and steamed suet sponge, a cake made with shredded beef fat instead of butter. The latter, when made by careless cooks, can turn into an edible boulder that would serve well as the foundation stone for a small building. Suet sponge has done more to damage the reputation of British food than almost any other dish, but only because critics had never tried my grandmother's. Hers was a crumbly cloud which, when combined with the syrup and thick cream, provided me with a definition of *delicious* that has lasted to this day. We would eat it in companionable silence, two friends at the opposite end of the same journey, joined together through food.

Between them, my mother and grandmother taught me to enjoy my meals, to be unafraid because they always tasted good—but it was my father who taught me that food was an adventure. Every Saturday evening, he would whisk us off to a restaurant where I would be exposed to some new "exotic" dish. Dad had only one rule—"try it first"—and I knew that, having done so, I would never be forced to eat anything I didn't want. He gave me confidence, patiently resetting my fingers time and again as my little hand struggled to control chopsticks, or ordering dozens of different curry dishes until we found the one with just the right amount of heat. I was five when he whisked us out of the country altogether—to Paris, where his newspaper had sent him as a foreign correspondent. It was his third tour of duty in this beautiful city and he took huge pleasure in introducing me to some of his favorite haunts.

At this point my childhood memories of food dissolve into a series of images: vacuuming up the most delicious onion soup at one in the morning in the old market of Les Halles, following an evening of fireworks and dancing in the streets on my first Quatorze Juillet (France's Independence Day); shooting shells across the table as I came to grip with snails, which tasted to me like bits of eraser in a gloriously garlicky butter sauce; or breaking le nez (the nose) off the impossibly long baguettes of French bread that my mother would buy hot from the boulangerie. I came to associate the places we traveled to with the food we ate, remembering fragrances and tastes, along with all the sights. Even now, certain names bring them immediately to mind:

• *Poland:* breakfasts of hard cheese, soft white rolls, and greengage jam, often the most appetizing meal of the day in a communist country that, even in 1963, was still recovering from the war.

- *North Africa:* couscous for lunch at the camel market in Nabeul, surrounded by biblical sights, pungent smells, and a mother trying to look casual.

- *Switzerland:* warm dinners of cheese fondue in the afterglow of après ski, following another bottom-numbing day on the nursery slopes.

It was wonderful training in so many ways, teaching me to be observant, flexible, and inquisitive about the world. We've tried to raise Charley in like vein, despite the fact that we now rarely travel. Our move down to the farm was number fifty-four in two lives that had been spent mostly on the road. We wanted our daughter to have more stability, but were also determined that her education wouldn't suffer. So we've mixed our parents' lessons with a few tricks of our own, whisking her to faraway spots through the combined magic of video, books, music, and an extensive culinary repertoire. Charley is now a veteran consumer of French, Italian, Indian, German, Greek, Hungarian, Thai, Mexican, Japanese, Chinese, Vietnamese, and, of course, British dishes. She has her inevitable list of dislikes, but she's usually willing to try. Like my father, that's all we ask, just keep an open mind. Be excited, be curious, because these are essential qualities for loving food—and for loving life.

Nana Moyce's Syrup Pudding

The two main ingredients in this recipe—the syrup and shred-ded suet—are surprisingly easy to find (in the Midwest, at least). Lyle's Golden Syrup is usually available at any good import store. The suet can be bought from your supermarket butcher—but you'll probably have to grate or shred it yourself.

1¼ cup all-purpose flour	⅓ cup light brown sugar
1 cup shredded suet	1 teaspoon nutmeg
1 teaspoon ground ginger	1 teaspoon baking soda
1 lemon	1 egg
salt	milk
6 tablespoons golden syrup	2-pint glass or ceramic bowl to
heavy cream	serve as a pudding basin
1½ cups breadcrumbs	

1. Dust suet with flour and grate by hand, using the larger holes on the grater. (Don't try this by machine because the suet will turn to mush.) 2. Finely grate the skin of the lemon, trying to avoid the white pith. 3. Grease a pudding basin with the but-ter. 4. In double saucepan or a small bowl set over a pan of boil-

ing water, melt the syrup. 5. Stir in the grated lemon rind. 6. Add 1 tablespoon of the warm syrup to the bottom of the pudding basin. 7. In a mixing bowl, combine the flour, breadcrumbs, spices, sugar, baking soda, and salt. 8. Beat the egg with 3 tablespoons of the warmed golden syrup and a tablespoon of milk. 9. Combine with the flour mixture and keep adding milk until the batter is of a soft dropping consistency. 10. Pour the mixture into the pudding basin. 11. Cover with a damp clean cloth and tie down firmly with string or a heavy-duty rubber band. 12. Set a cereal bowl or saucer in a steamer or large saucepan. 13. Half fill with water. 14. Bring the water to the boil. 15. Set the pudding basin in the pan. 16. Steam for 2 hours, making sure that the pan does not boil dry. 17. Warm the rest of the syrup. 18. Serve over the pudding, with a whirl of heavy cream.

One Man's Meat...

HAVE TO ADMIT THAT I STARTED IT, BUT GREG should really share the blame. It was early in our relationship and he'd been showing off his firsthand knowledge of Far Eastern cuisine by ordering special dishes at every Chinese restaurant we went to. With a dismissive look on his face, he'd set the menu aside and speak in low tones to the waiter. "Can I have wonton soup?" he'd ask conspiratorially, "with Cantonese-style egg noodles? I'd also like some pork fried rice, with green onions, white onions, bean sprouts, and egg—but no peas or carrots. You know, Chinese style." Our hosts would look surprised, impressed, sometimes a little baffled, but his next question would always rock them on their heels. "And if you have any lapchong hidden out in the kitchen, could we have some steamed?"

"Lapchong?" they'd hiss, as if Greg had discovered some state secret. "How do you know about lapchong?" Then he'd charm and tease them into bringing us a plate of this delicious Chinese sausage, poached in a dark, sweet soy sauce.

Now we were in San Francisco, headed for an adventure in its famous Chinatown. We arrived at the restaurant just as the owners themselves were sitting down to eat, and my eye was drawn to the large porcelain bowl in front of them. It was piled high with shells, the delicate spirals I was so used to from France: they were eating snails. I nudged Greg. "Look! Mm, yummy, let's order some." He was about to protest when the waiter materialized by our table. "Could we have a portion of those?" I asked, pointing at the dish. He stepped over to consult his boss. Our host's face split into a huge grin, then he nodded vigorously and waved in our direction. I settled back, slightly smug at having found something that Greg had never tried.

When our meal arrived, the snails were brought out last in an even bigger bowl than the one in front of the owner's family. I peeked over its edge, expecting the fragrance of garlic and, possibly, ginger to fill my nostrils. Instead, my heart froze. These weren't the innocuous French invertebrates, raised on some pristine farm; these were street snails in all their slimy reality, so robust that they still seemed to be wriggling in their shells. Greg's eyes started to dance as he pushed the bowl over to my side of the booth. . . .

Open-mindedness aside, there are some foods that I simply cannot bring myself to eat. A few—a very few—make my black list purely on the basis of taste (lentil soup, well-hung game of any kind, and refried beans, which, I think, look and smell like cat-sick). Other dishes are more a matter of crossing some personal or cultural taboo. My friends from Hong Kong can extol the virtues of snake as much as they please, but I prefer to eat the chicken that they say it tastes so much like. I was equally dubious about the fried grasshoppers munched on by Fernando, my driver when I was in Mexico reporting on the earthquake; and nearly disgraced myself one evening when he told me that the salsa we were eating was made with jumiles—which are known better to us as stinkbugs. It's an irrational prejudice, considering that they are just smaller arthropods, members of the same family as the wonderful lobster and shrimp, but my stomach rebelled spontaneously when it discovered I was feeding it insects. It also heaves at the thought of eating dog, a common practice throughout the

Pacific rim. I understand that the relationship between human and canine in these areas is not at all the same and that the Western closeness to dogs is actually regarded as bizarre—but, with absolute respect for our differences, I decline to eat someone who, under other circumstances, might have been my friend.

I feel the same way about the parrots that are being consumed in such quantity throughout South America. As I write this a gray cockatiel sits on the back of my chair. Her name is Sweetie Pie and her little body houses more personality than many people I know. She teases, fusses, loves, and sulks if she feels neglected. She will rattle the bars of her cage when she wants to come out and will put herself away when she's had enough, slamming the door behind her. Parrots are even more social and have been known to suffer from mental breakdowns when not shown enough affection. They are at the opposite end of the sentient scale from chickens, who, I can personally attest, raise stupidity to a new numbness. So although parrots may be more prolific than chickens in certain parts of the world, it would break my heart to eat one.

There's no judgment implied in these prejudices—quite the reverse. The fault is mine for not caring that many bugs contain more protein than prime beef, or that the flesh of reptiles would be good for my incipient arthritis. I just prefer, when given the choice, to be selective about local culinary customs. That even applies at home, where squirrel stew and baked possum are consumed enthusiastically by several of our neighbors, who add to their larders throughout the year by hunting the different animals in season. Making the most of the land's resources is the country way, but the furthest I get is to catch our own fish. If the supermarkets closed tomorrow, I'd probably change, but for now I'll buy my meat from the butcher, while borrowing from Voltaire: "I may not like what you eat, but I'll defend to the death your right to eat it. . . ."

This is not so when animals die for humanity's ego or greed. As a child, I was appalled by stories of banquets in ancient Rome, where hundreds of flamingos died to provide a dish of tiny tongues, or equal numbers of peacocks were slaughtered for that admired Roman status symbol, a bowl of peacocks' brains. The decimation of all that beauty for such passing self-indulgence seemed to me a mortal sin, a symbol of a cruel and corrupt society that contained within it the seeds of its own destruction.

Today, I save my anger for more contemporary abominations. We appear to have learned little across the centuries and still need to eat the exotic as proof of our power or wealth. In the

West, the glitterati try to revive their jaded palates by hunting dolphin in the Caribbean or purchasing delicacies like elephant's trunk and smoked bear from some of Europe's finest food emporiums. In Africa, the latest fad from the Cameroon and Congo is the meat of the endangered great ape. Monkeys have been hunted for centuries in these areas, but most of the animals were able to live safely in the region's vast forests. Now logging companies from Europe are cutting their habitat down, bringing the poachers in behind them to kill gorillas and chimpanzees by the thousands. They're not hunting for their own food, they're killing for consumers in the cities who enjoy this new delicacy so much that they will pay three times the price they pay for fillet steak. In Malaysia, similar devastation is being wrought on the little sun bear—the smallest and rarest of his kind. These charming creatures are cuddly toys come to life, who spend their years innocently roaming the rain forests in search of the fruit and honey they love to eat. This diet is what makes their flesh so sweet, although connoisseurs claim that it's at its best when the bears die in agony. . . .

These obscenities are, for the most part, illegal, but history has taught us that dietary laws never work unless they are teamed with society's support. It's going to require a real shift in people's values, a redefinition of what we mean by the word *luxury,* before humankind finds eating the rare and beautiful as revolting as I found those Chinese snails.

I did try, not wishing to offend our enthusiastic host. I hid them in spring rolls and wrapped them in rice—but it was no good, I couldn't force them down. Greg did nothing to relieve my suffering until the end of the meal, when he beckoned the waiter over. "A delicious dinner"—he beamed—"but we're really full. Could we wrap the rest to go?" The waiter nodded, unperturbed, and came back in a few minutes with several boxes. The owner saw us off, still smiling, to my great relief. The following morning I walked down to the bay, where I fed the snails to the seagulls, who screamed out their delight.

Cantonese Fried Rice

Very few people know how to cook this properly anymore. The younger generation of chefs coming over to America from Hong Kong and Shanghai have bowed to our prejudices about health and abandoned the seasonings that make this dish so special.

Bead molasses and thick dark soy sauce should be available at most specialty food-stores.

2 cups steamed long-grain
   white rice
3–4 tablespoons corn oil
2–3 tablespoons bead molasses
4 tablespoons dark,
   thick soy sauce
2 cups diced cooked Chinese
   barbecued pork with any
   fat cut off. (This can be
   bought from a local Chinese
   restaurant, where it might
   also be called char sui pork.)
   Or 2 cups of cooked chicken,
   beef, or shrimp may be
   substituted.

1 cup fresh bean sprouts
⅔ cup chopped green onion
3 medium-size eggs

1. Have all the ingredients, cleaned and prepared, waiting by the side of wok or electric skillet. 2. Heat 2 1/2 tablespoons of the corn oil. 3. Break the eggs into a bowl and partially scramble

them with a fork. 4. Pour the eggs onto the hot oil. 5. Keep breaking the cooking egg up into small pieces. When they are cooked, push them to the side of the wok. 6. Add the rice, bead molasses, and soy sauce and combine well with the egg. (Make sure that the rice is well coated with the seasonings.) 7. Add the bean sprouts, pork (or the chicken, beef, or shrimp) and an additional 1 1/2 tablespoons of oil. 8. Continue stir-frying until throughly heated through.

Old Mother Hubbard

HE SINK HAD BEEN DROPPING HEAVY HINTS
for days — bubbly hiccups warning that the septic
tank was nearly full. I chose to ignore it. March can
be a difficult month for us, when every penny must be stretched.
It's the height of the slow season in Greg's photography business,
which always hits just as last season's food supplies are running
out. Cash flow can be touch and go, and at that moment a
plumber's bill was the last thing we needed.

It was a mistake. Two days later, after a couple of spring
storms, the now-familiar belch was followed by a rushing sound

and ice-cold "black water" spurted like a geyser from the plug hole. We had the tank pumped immediately, but the sink continued to back up, leading us to the horrible conclusion that the main drainage pipe was blocked. Four hundred dollars later our sewage was safely on its way again and we were left with the small problem of how to feed ourselves until the next check came in. The joys of being self-employed . . .

I used to panic about tight times. My throat would be seized by an invisible hand that made swallowing and breathing a conscious effort until we were back on an even keel. Then, a few years ago, I heard someone quote a text I learned as a child but had never really listened to before. Perhaps one needs to have lived a bit to appreciate that the wisdom and truth contained in the Sermon on the Mount applies to all, no matter what their faith or philosophy:

> "Therefore I tell you, do not worry about your life, what you will eat or what you will drink, or about your body, what you will wear. Is not life more than food, and the body more than clothing? Look at the birds of the air; they neither sow nor reap nor gather into barns, and yet your heavenly Father feeds them. Are you not of more value than they? And can any of you by worrying add a single hour to your span of life?"

We would survive—we always had—and were usually the better for it. Living on an impossible budget can even be a game that has led to some of our happiest memories and most creative cooking.

At times like these, we begin by taking inventory in the kitchen to ensure that the essentials are in stock. Each household is different and it depends on what you eat, but I know that if we have the following, meals won't be a problem:

Flour	Rice	Garlic	Pepper	Chicken
Sugar	Pasta	Oil	Paprika	Cheese
Salt	Potatoes	Butter	Nutmeg	
Milk	Tomatoes	Yeast	Cinnamon	
Eggs	Onions	Vinegar	Bacon	

Having taken stock, we then draw up a plan based on the number of meals needed and the money available. Finally, we make a list and go shopping. There are certain rules about this: don't buy any preprepared foods; put at least 25 percent of available funds into fresh vegetables and fruit; and never come home with anything that will make just one dish. Thus, with thirty-four dollars and ninety-seven cents, we were able to get a six-pound roasting capon, two pounds of cheddar, a pack of bacon, five pounds of apples, tomatoes (fresh and canned), celery, green beans, lettuce, a cabbage, a cauliflower, five pounds of potatoes, two gallons of milk, lemons, and a bag of oranges—in other words, a week's worth of breakfasts, lunches, and dinners for a family of three. That may seem like an unlikely equation, but with a little help from the farm it wasn't even a stretch.

Day One fell on a Saturday, so we devoted our time to cooking for the week ahead. These concentrated sessions in the kitchen are communal events that are usually reserved for the holidays. A pot of tea sits constantly ready on the stove and music murmurs in the background as the family pitches in together, hands working busily while the conversation flows. On this occasion, I baked up a batch of white bread and a large apple tart, and mixed crusts for a quiche and a pot pie, while Greg and Charley prepared a week's vegetables and grated enough cheese to make a quart of sauce that would later be adapted for "cheesy pasta" and fondue. We had roast capon that night, with roast potatoes and green beans. When we'd finished, I picked the bird clean, setting aside enough meat for two more meals. The carcass was put into our big stock pot with an onion, a couple of carrots, salt, pepper, a bay leaf, and a bunch of wild garlic from the pasture. This was left to simmer overnight on the lowest of heats. In the morning, I strained the broth into a clean glass storage jar, which cooled on the kitchen counter while Charley and I preempted Easter with an early egg hunt.

Our chickens had started to pay their rent again, responding to the height of the sun in the sky rather than the raw and windy weather. They don't make collection easy, however. A few cooperative souls lay in the boxes we built for them, but most hide their clutches then wander off, leaving the forgotten nest to fester in some dark corner like a time bomb under the straw. These were what we were looking for, stepping gingerly to avoid the earsplitting explosion of a broken rotten egg that always precedes that most legendary of smells. . . .

We raise Aracana hens—also known as "Easter egg chicks" because they produce eggs with the most beautifully colored shells, ranging from olive green and turquoise blue to a delicate blush pink. Their content is the same as any other from a free-range hen: a firm white and a deep orange-yellow yolk, with a taste that's about as far removed from the store-bought variety as vintage champagne is from ditch water. Murphey chickens are particularly spoiled. They're fed the best, then allowed to roam the farm at will, picking at delicacies in the grass or gossiping around the compost pile in self-satisfied groups, smug in the knowledge that they'll die of old age. It may not be good husbandry, but they repay us by moving across the lawn like liquid art—and by continuing to supply us with one of nature's most versatile foods long after other hens retire. We store their gifts in the refrigerator point down, where they will stay fresh for twelve weeks or more. When we run out of room, we break the surplus into individual ice trays and freeze them. The resulting "egg cubes" are packed in plastic bags and will be perfectly edible for the next nine months, although they don't taste as rich as eggs that are used on the day they are laid. These freshest-of-the-fresh add buttery depth to everything from mayonnaise to the common omelette, and even the whites bring something extra to meringues and soufflés. The treasure that Charley and I collected that morning enabled the family to feast on delights like avgolemono (the Greek egg-and-lemon sauce), peppery frittatas, and paper-thin crêpes suzettes drenched in orange butter. They also provided sweet clouds of zabaglione, one of my favorite desserts, on the day we cooked a special Italian meal to celebrate being solvent again.

It was nice to have peace of mind, but as we sat down to our minestrone I knew that prosperity comes at a price. The next day we'd go grocery shopping to buy more expensive but easier food that required less time and preparation. The triumph of con-

cocting something wonderful each night would soon disappear
as meals were fitted in once more around the work we do to earn
the funds we need to pay the bills and buy the food we eat to fuel
the work that we do. It's a tight circle, designed more for ham-
sters than for human beings. Our only chance of breaking it was
to remember that the time we had just spent so happily together
had enriched us in a way than money never could. . . .

Zabaglione

This recipe looks deceptively simple, but it requires attention to
detail and a sense of timing to get it right. At its best, a *zabaglione*
should be halfway between liquid and solid—a warm froth that
stands stiffly on the spoon, but melts when it touches the mouth.
I think the four essentials for success are: 1. That the egg yolks
are at room temperature. 2. That all the cups, spoons, etc., are
ready by the stove before you start, having been washed in hot
water so they are warm. 3. That you make the *zabaglione* in a
double saucepan. And 4. That it is served the second it is done.

*2 egg yolks, 1 heaping
teaspoon of light brown
sugar, and 1 tablespoon of
Marsala wine per person*

1 biscotti *or sponge
finger per serving*

1. Bring the water in the double saucepan to a boil, then re-duce to a simmer over a low heat. 2. Whip the yolks and the sugar together with an eggbeater until they are frothy. 3. Beat in the Marsala. 4. Pour the mixture into the top half of the saucepan, beating continuously: do not allow it to boil. 5. The mixture should froth up. When it has crested, it is ready to serve. If the yolks start to coagulate, remove the pan from the heat immediately, beating all the while. 6. Serve preferably in glass cappuccino cups with a sponge finger or *biscotti* on the side.

Details, Details . . .

HE *NOISETTES* OF LAMB APPEARED TO HAVE been marinated in soy and garlic, then glazed in something sweet before they were sautéed. I asked our hostess what it was. "I have no idea." She tittered. "I can't boil water. . . ." The statement was made with an undertone of pride, suggesting that she was far too sophisticated to be caught dead in a kitchen. My jaw muscles clenched; I'm getting awfully tired of women who express their emancipation through their unwillingness to cook.

The fact is that there's nothing liberated about rejecting what is, at its best, one of the arts and, at its very least, an expression of our humanity. Cooking a meal of any kind is an easy way to fulfil the creativity that lurks within us all. I have much more patience with those who say they can't, rather than won't cook, because they are not pretentious: they are merely wrong. Everyone can, it's simply a question of paying attention to the details.

These fall into three categories: preparation, execution, and presentation. Let's begin with preparation. The old saying " you can't make a silk purse out of a sow's ear" sums it up—good food depends on having good raw materials. I don't know how many dinners I've been to where a wonderful sauce has been spoiled by a cheap cut of meat, or at least meat that hasn't been cooked for long enough. You can always tell because it tastes gamy and takes forever to chew through. Dishes like Stroganoff or beef bourguignon are at their best when made with filet or sirloin. If you insist on using chuck or flank, you must balance economy with time. The meat will need to stew for hours— preferably after having been marinated first.

Similar principles apply to vegetables and fruit. Greg and I are used to the strange looks we get in grocery stores when we sniff the base of pineapples or spend fifteen minutes sorting through the strawberries. A ripening pineapple should smell like one and give just a little to the touch. Strawberries should be free of blemishes, fairly uniform in color, and firm without being hard. If you get a woody one by accident, it's important to cut out the core and save the sweet flesh around it. We wash and dry each one of ours individually, then spritz them with lemon juice and a sprinkling of maple syrup. Served with crème chantilly (thick cream whipped with vanilla and sugar), they are a dessert fit for a king.

Flavor also depends on the way fruit and vegetables are cut. Texture plays as important a part as taste in good cooking, either leaving ingredients in the background or bringing them to the fore. An onion diced into tiny pieces is an entirely different animal from one that has been roughly chopped. The first almost liquefies in a broth, providing an underlying kick to the main flavors. The second thrusts itself forward—not as a support player, but as one of the stars. Greg can cut vegetables more finely than anyone I know. He's very finicky about it—in fact, he is most particular about food preparation in general. This is the man who will spend an hour trimming every piece of gristle and fat out of the meat for his spaghetti sauce; the cook who claims to be able to tell the difference between tap water and distilled; the husband who will carefully pick the white membrane out of eggs that he's about to scramble for breakfast. I've always found this last to be bordering on the obsessive, but I'm forced—reluctantly—to admit that it does make the eggs taste better.

Our different approaches to the preparation of food are typical, in some ways, of the contrast between the ways that men and women live. When I make dinner, it's usually only one task among the many I'm taking care of: turn the oven on; start the laundry; season and sear the meat; help with Charley's homework; call the plumber; clean the mushrooms; and so on. . . . When it's Greg's turn at the stove, he is utterly absorbed by the work at hand. A tornado could hit the house, but he probably wouldn't notice as long as the kitchen was left standing.

My domestic juggling act will sound familiar to many modern women, as will the mistakes that result occasionally from my not concentrating. The great Julia Child's cure-all of "throwing a sauce on it" works with some calamities, but I've also had to learn that curdling mayonnaise can be stopped with a drop of vinegar and sugar; or that stubborn egg whites will stand smartly to attention with the addition of a pinch of salt; or that over-salted food can be calmed by adding a peeled potato to the brew. All you need is a little imagination and the courage to experiment to build up a food first-aid kit of your own. I've only ever had one accident that was beyond rescue—the gravy for a roast chicken that I'd thickened with confectioners' sugar instead of flour. . . .

Modern life also runs smoother for those who develop a series of kitchen shortcuts. Mine include always cooking freezable dishes three dinners at a time; inventing an all-purpose salad dressing that will survive life in a large bottle kept in the refrigerator; and prepreparing vegetables and salad on the day that they are bought, then storing them in individual airtight boxes so that they are immediately to hand. These three measures alone have ensured that the family gets decent food on the most frenetic day, and I haven't even touched on the meals that can be put together in minutes. Many of these will impress the sternest critic if a little planning has been put into their presentation.

I was once asked to design a menu for a colleague who was convinced she couldn't cook. Sue was a dedicated TV reporter whose whole life had been her career, until she met a man and fell in love. They had spent the first few months of their relationship eating out, but now he had invited himself over for lunch because he "had something important to discuss." She was terrified that a culinary disaster would dampen his enthusiasm and turned to me for help. Romantic encounters are generally not good for the appetite, so we settled on light fare that could be eaten easily, without awkward tools or a sauce that might dribble unattractively down someone's chin. The appetizer would be smoked salmon, dressed with lime juice, cracked black pepper, and capers, and served on whole wheat toast that had been spread with sweet butter and cut into pretty shapes with a cookie cutter. This would be followed by large bowls of moules marinières—that magical concoction of fresh mussels, white wine, onions, and herbs that can be a complete meal when eaten with crusty hunks of hot French bread. The recipe is simplicity itself. The only thing to watch out for, as I warned Sue, is that the shellfish are thoroughly clean. This is best accomplished by soaking them in ice water overnight, with the cold tap running slowly into one side of the bowl—the constant flow will wash away any grit and sand. In the morning, the mussels should be put into fresh water and kept in the refrigerator.

Sue never did get to dessert (mixed berries chantilly, garnished with shaved chocolate), her lover proposed after the light green salad. She still works in television today, carefully balancing her successful public life with two beautiful children and a husband who boasts proudly about his wife's abilities in the kitchen. . . .

Indeed, I'll be sending Sue the recipe for those *noisettes* of lamb that we enjoyed so much at dinner. After we'd finished, I went in search of the true founder of the feast. Our caterer turned out to be little more than a girl with downy cheeks still flushed from heat and exertion. She had glazed the lamb in red currant jelly, she told me, "It's pretty easy." But the work must be hard, I commiserated. "Oh, no . . . I love it." She beamed. "And business is booming. . . ."

Moules Marinières

I'm delighted to see bags of these shellfish appearing recently in local supermarkets, because nothing could be easier to prepare. You just have to remember that these are live creatures and will respond accordingly. Begin by scraping off any seaweed, beards, and barnacles, before soaking them in the bowl of ice water. Any mussels that float to the top should be thrown away, along with any broken or partly open shells that don't snap shut when you tap them with a knife. A fresh mussel should be firmly closed until it's cooked. Finally, clean the mussels in cold running water as already described. I allow about a pint of shellfish per person if they are being served as an appetizer, and a quart per person if they are the main dish.

4 quarts mussels	*4 cups dry white wine*
2 large cloves garlic	*1 bay leaf*
1 small bunch thyme	*2 sprigs of tarragon*
Salt & fresh ground	*1 small bunch parsley*
* black pepper*	

1. Clean the mussels the night before. 2. Crush the garlic. 3. Heat the wine, garlic, and herbs in a deep saucepan that has a lid, over a medium-to-low heat. 4. Season the liquor to taste with the salt and fresh pepper. 5. Add the mussels, cover the pan, and shake gently for a few minutes as the mussels cook. 6. The mussels are ready when the shells are open. Discard the herbs and serve the mussels in large soup bowls with the liquid they were cooked in and garnished with chopped parsley. You will also need plenty of French bread to sop up the delicious juices!

Crème Chantilly

This classic dessert topping goes well with everything from fruit salad to chocolate mousse. It also lends itself to a number of interesting variations: I sometimes replace the vanilla with a few drops of orange-blossom oil and sprinkle the top with very finely grated orange peel; or I blend fresh raspberries into a pulp and fold them into the whipped cream. Both ways make an interesting change, but I have to admit that the original recipe is still the best:

1 pint heavy whipping cream
1 tablespoon superfine sugar

1 capful vanilla extract
(please use the real thing; the substitute doesn't taste the same)

1. Refrigerate the cream overnight. 2. If you are using a food processor, make sure that the bowl and blade are free from oil and absolutely dry. Whip the cream and the sugar together. 3. When the cream will stand in soft peaks, beat in the vanilla. 4. Refrigerate again before serving.

The Price of Milk

LL THESE STORIES HAVE PROBABLY LED YOU to believe that I'm a mix between Martha Stewart and Daniel Boone—a rural superwoman, holding down her work while running a home that belongs in *Country Life* and a table fit for the pages of *Bon Appétit*. Nothing could be further from the truth. Writers try to tell their best stories, using their funniest events, most moving moments, their deepest thoughts—with the result that the reader gets all of the yin and little, if any, of the yang.

The reality is that we spend many evenings eating soup and salad or beans and franks, and are certainly not above picking up a pizza on our way home. I've been caught drinking straight out of a bottle from the refrigerator and find the idea of putting doilies on lamb chops faintly quaint. When both Greg and I are working hard, the housework gets shoved to the bottom of the list. You can measure exactly how busy I am by the piles of clothes waiting to be washed and the clouds of pet hair gathering in the corners.

Ten years ago I wouldn't have made such admissions to myself, let alone in print, but that was when I still subscribed to one of the great illusions of our age: that I could be it all—devoted mother, perfect wife, and consummate career woman. Our move to the farm was supposed to cure that, but initially I just added one more role to the list. Now I had to be the capable country woman, too—growing or raising all our own food from the immaculate barns and gardens surrounding our beautifully restored stone cottage, that would always be filled with the mingled fragrances of flowers and home cooking.

It was an impossible—even undesirable—dream, but I didn't know that until we started keeping goats. . . .

Greg never wanted them, but I was determined. After all, how self-sufficient can you claim to be without producing your own milk? Milk is so basic to life. It's our first food, utterly complete in both the nutritional and emotional senses. Its very name provokes an almost visceral response: "mother's milk," "the milk of human kindness," "a land of milk and honey" are sayings replete with feelings of comfort and plenty. Milk speaks to us of safety and gentleness, so that even the many adults who are lactose-intolerant yearn for what they perceive as its soothing balm on the stomach. The idea of spending each airbrushed dawn peacefully milking the cow seemed to me an essential part of country living and I was disappointed to discover, after we moved, that a cow would produce more in a morning than our family consumed in a month. The obvious alternative was a less abundant animal—i.e., a goat.

I began with an experienced nanny called Libby and a little buck we named Henry. The idea was that Henry would grow up and mate with Libby, resulting in kids for us to raise or sell and a regular supply of the white stuff. For the first few months it went well. The animals seemed content with their new home, were affectionate with us, and soon became firm members of the family. In the fall, when Henry grew tall enough to reach, the two of them consummated their relationship and Libby gave birth to adorable twins the following spring. At this point things started to go sour.

As the babies grew it became clear that both were "intellectually challenged." The male, Max, was so stupid he could barely stand upright, while the female, Celine, was an utter sociopath. Unfortunately, this aggression rubbed off on her mother and Libby developed a distinctly chilly attitude toward us just about the time she was ready to be milked.

She communicated this need one afternoon when she followed me down the fence line bleating unhappily, with udders the size of zeppelins. I was unprepared, but this was clearly an emergency and had to be dealt with on the spot. Charley was delegated to hold Libby's head while I worked at the other end into a kitchen stockpot. The moment my hands made contact, the goat took off, drop-kicking the pot and dragging my daughter behind her. We started over, this time with me holding her collar, while I tried to milk her one-handed. She bucked and shied, and a strong stream of milk shot out and hit Charley in the eye. On our third attempt, I straddled her back and reached down to relieve her overabundance. Libby took off again and I found myself riding her around the pasture backward, with one hand firmly clamped on to her teat. . . .

Our neighbor, Big John, came to my rescue with lessons and an old milking stand he'd built, but it was too late: Libby already knew that she had the upper hoof. Each session became a battle of wills that began with a Chaplinesque struggle to get her onto the stand and usually ended with an overturned bucket or the milk polluted by a hairy, mud-soaked foot. I don't know who was more relieved when Libby dried up that November in preparation for another mating—but I was certainly the most disillusioned. I spent the winter months reading books on the subject, in the hope of improving matters come the spring.

I discovered that I had underrated dairying as a skill. Producing fine milk (of any kind) can be like producing fine wine—a delicate balance between one's basic stock, what it's fed, how its fruits are harvested, and how they are nursed through their final stages. (Some French cheese makers say that there are good growths—*crus*—for milk, just as there are for wine.) In Europe, goat's milk commands as much respect as a cow's. Contrary to American popular belief, it isn't musky or rank but can taste even sweeter than its bovine equivalent—as long as it is absolutely fresh and handled under very clean conditions. Its natural flavor will be even further enhanced if the nanny's diet is carefully balanced and she's given extra treats like herbs, apples, or bee balm (which comes through in the milk as a faint under-taste of honey).

The digestibility of goat's milk is not a myth. It is richer in but-terfat than cow's milk, but the globules are smaller and more evenly spread through the liquid. It is naturally homogenized, if you like, which is why it is so sought after by sufferers of stom-ach complaints. It is also why I, despite my first season's lamen-table performance, was determined to carry on. Greg had had terrible gastric problems ever since a surgery in 1993 and I was convinced that our own goat's milk—along with the cheeses and yogurt we would make from it—could only help his health.

By the time Libby was in milk again the following May, I was ready for her. A kitchen shelf had been set aside for the stainless-steel pail, glass jars, strainers, strip cups, brushes, and filters that would be needed each day; the milk stand had been scrubbed and bleached; and Libby had been bathed and shaved in all the right places. Every morning just after dawn, I sterilized all the equip-ment, went out to the barn, got the goat on to the stand (still a struggle), washed her udders, tied her back leg down so she couldn't kick the bucket, spent half an hour milking her, turned her loose, took the milk back to the house, where it was strained through several filters before being decanted into the sterile jars and pasteurized in a water bath at 165 degrees. The entire procedure was repeated again in the evening, because goats do better when they're milked twice a day. . . . It took about a month for me to realize the enormous amount of time being spent on this one task.

At first, I ignored it. I can be quite stubborn and was, in any case, much too proud of the full jars in the refrigerator and of the *chèvre* rolled in cracked pepper, or the yogurt I was learning to make from them. But after a while even I had to confess that the cheese tasted mediocre, the yogurt often wouldn't set, and the milking had turned into a relentless routine that felt more like a prison sentence than a pastoral pursuit. The enterprise didn't make economic sense, either: three hours of effort every day to produce two gallons of finished milk meant that each gallon was costing roughly thirty dollars. Throw in the goats' feed, equipment, and the time spent in caretaking, and the figure was closer to fifty! But it was Greg who really put an end to it all by announcing that he wouldn't drink another drop because he couldn't "get past where it came from."

What is life if we don't learn from its experiences? As we watched their silly faces bounce off in a trailer on their way to a real farm, I realized how much the goats had taught me.

I no longer believed that home-raised or homemade food was automatically better, and had developed a deep respect for the dairymen and cheese makers who devote a lifetime to their craft. Our ability to buy Feta from Greece or Stilton from Wisconsin is one of the blessings of our age, a hallmark of a society rich in cultural resources. While the humble gallon of milk—a wonder of the modern world—is a symbol of how far we've come since our foremothers' time. It has given us the gift of freedom—precious extra hours every day that we can choose to spend either on impossible images of perfection or on the complicated process of simply being ourselves.

Vinegar Cheese

Even though we don't make our own dairy products anymore, it's still fun to know how. Charley and I refresh our memories, every now and then, by making this simple vinegar cream cheese. Its texture and taste lend themselves well to being mixed with fresh herbs and crushed garlic, or finely chopped sun-dried tomatoes, or even crushed blackberries and honey for an unusual sweet spread.

Equipment

   1 enamel, stainless-steel   *1 colander*
      or glass saucepan   *cheesecloth*
      (do not use aluminum)   *a bowl*
   1 thermometer

   I gallon whole milk   *salt*
   ¼ cup white vinegar

1. Heat the milk slowly until it reaches 185 degrees. 2. Stir in the vinegar. 3. Bring the temperature back to 185 degrees and keep it there, stirring occasionally, until a soft curd has formed. (This will take about 15 minutes.) 4. Line the colander with the cheesecloth. 5. Pour the curd onto the cloth. 6. Sprinkle with salt. 7. Tie the opposite corners of the cloth together into a bundle, then hang the cheese up to drain overnight. (I usually attach it to a cabinet doorknob, but a cup hook would do—anywhere it can hang free.) 8. In the morning, turn the cheese into a bowl and mix in whatever seasonings strike your fancy. 9. Form the cheese into a block and press between 2 plates with a weight on top. 10. Refrigerate for a few hours. It is now ready to eat. If it is kept covered in a refrigerator, it will stay fresh for about a week.

A Cloth of Many Colors

UST LOOK AT ALL THIS!" MY FATHER GAZED down the groaning rows of goods on the supermarket shelves. "Charley's certainly getting a multicultural education." It was his first visit to the farm and he'd arrived with some of the vague preconceptions that Europeans have about the States. We are seen as a "meat and potatoes" people who exist mainly on fast food, and he was surprised and pleased to find that goods from around the world were available even at our regional store.

Dad is much more open-minded than many from across the

pond who like to dismiss America as the brash kid on the block, the teenager with more money than sense, able to acquire endlessly without discrimination. To them, we are a country with little cultural tradition—a child at the dining table of history who is better seen and not heard. In these circles, "American cuisine" is an oxymoron: we are give none of the credit and all of the blame for developments in modern food.

This nonsense has been going on ever since the Europeans co-opted that most American of birds and called it the turkey, the calecutischer hahn (Calcutta hen) or le dinde (as in d'Inde—from India). It was as if they couldn't bear to admit that the Colonies could be home to anything so delicious. On the other hand, they have no problem accusing us of inventing such vulgarities as the doggie bag or the food vending machine, despite the facts that the former has long been used in France, where such estimable gourmets as Alexandre Dumas were known for packing up part of dinner and sending it 'round to friends, while the latter was invented by the Swedish. . . . It is true that America's culinary tradition is different from theirs, but that's merely a reflection of its history.

American cuisine is a cloth of many colors. Each culture that has settled here has laid down one strand, bright in its own right, but brighter still when it overlaps with others to form a new pattern in the weave. Thus the Native Americans gave msiquatash to our Pilgrim fathers, who added cream, black pepper, and bacon to it, turning it into the succotash we would recognize today. When the recipe traveled south, okra, tomatoes, and nutmeg found their way into it; when it traveled west, the Pennsylvania Dutch added potatoes and green peppers. This kind of cross-fertilization has happened all around the country. In that capital of good cooking, New Orleans, the classic Creole dish, gumbo, owes its name to an African word for okra, which has become a staple ingredient of the recipe—along with filé powder, a seasoning made from sassafras leaves by the Choctaw Indians. Gumbo wouldn't be gumbo without either of these two things, making it a truly multicultural food. Southern cooking in general has a lot to thank our African-American brethren for—from the use of black-eyed peas and peanuts to the introduction of the sesame seed, which was brought over by the slaves. It all depends on who settled, or was settled, where. Midwestern food is a mixture of its German, English, Scandinavian, Polish, and Dutch heritage; Californian cuisine is based heavily on influences from Asia and from Spain; while the fiery dishes of the Southwest are a perfect synthesis of their Mexican, Spanish, and Native American ancestors.

The joy of eating in the States is that you never know what delights are waiting for you just around the corner. We've had some truly wonderful meals in the most unlikely places. The best Southwestern food I've ever eaten, for instance, was at a seemingly anonymous hole-in-the-wall outside Albuquerque, New Mexico. Half-Breed Pete's was hidden along the Turquoise Trail on the way to Santa Fe. It may not have been mentioned in any of the guidebooks, but it was justly famous among its local clientele. The food was supreme. We dined there every night of our stay, as if the repetition could somehow fix all those sunny tastes in our memories for the long trip north: the sweet golden puffs of dough called sopaipillas (which are served as a first course in New Mexico with jugs of dark honey); the most deliciously seasoned fajitas (of both beef and chicken varieties) that Greg or I had ever tasted; the chiles rellenos; the enchiladas; even the bowls of velvet-smooth flan we had for dessert, would have given the best European eateries a run for their money. We haven't sampled the like since—despite all the fancy Southwestern restaurants that have sprung up nationwide.

The same could be said for the Thai food we've enjoyed at Arun's in Chicago, where Arun uses the freshest ingredients to re-create dishes eaten by the royal family of Siam; or the Tandoori meals, cooked in traditional clay ovens, at the India Garden in Indianapolis; or the classical German cuisine that has been served for generations at Ray Radigan's outside Kenosha, Wisconsin. They all have different national roots, but their raw materials, the tastes of their clientele, their very locations, make them American, too, and part of this country's culinary cloth.

When I first arrived in the States, I joined other Europeans in bemoaning the lack of local delicacies: there were no little towns that had spent generations refining one recipe for spice cake or pâté. Now that I'm more informed, I understand that while this may be so in fact, the spirit of the criticism is unfair. Americans are too young and too fluid a people to have developed such fixed customs, but each American state grows, raises, or produces special foods it can be truly proud of. Alaskan king salmon, Wisconsin cheeses, and Virginia ham are all obvious choices, but we must not forget white truffles from Oregon, maple syrup from Vermont, or pit-barbecued pork from Memphis, Tennessee. And what about blueberry pie or lobsters from Maine, Maryland crab cakes, Iowa pork, a Texas T-bone, New England clam chowder, catfish from Alabama, or Florida's key-lime pie? I don't have the space here to list every American delicacy, but even if I did, I couldn't hope to include all the hidden treasures—the preserves, pickles, pies, and sauces—that have yet to make it over their local county line. In time Aunt Bea's pepper jelly may well find its way on to the supermarket shelves. Another joy of living here is the ever-growing range of edible goods that is made available to us all around the country.

When Europeans visit us now, we give them the same advice about both America and its food: "Don't be deceived by appearances." That boisterous man in the lime green pants could easily be a pastor or a prizewinning poet and that anonymous tavern in a shabby strip mall may serve the best steak or peach cobbler you've ever tasted. Greg, who could find somewhere good to eat in the middle of a desert, says that he never judges a restaurant by its exterior or decor. He judges it by the number of cars in its parking lot. Sometimes you have to step back from this cloth to see the pictures hidden in its pattern—the bright images of a nation rich in different foods and a pioneering people who are still matching this and mixing that into a whole new series of culinary traditions.

Brown County Apple Butter & Biscuits

Since we're on the subject, I'm going to take this opportunity to introduce the wider world to a speciality from Brown County: apple butter and biscuits. As with *sopaipillas,* they are served before the meal—which made me, initially, most suspicious! They are, however, a delicious accompaniment to fall and winter food—or eaten on their own at breakfast. The recipes are mine, but they are the synthesis of wisdom collected from around the county. I would like to thank all the ladies who were so generous with their secrets:

Apple Butter—Ingredients

2 gallons of applesauce	½ cup ground cinnamon
1 teaspoon lemon juice	¼ cup ground cloves
¾ gallon hot water	6 cups sugar

1. Mix all the ingredients together and bake at 350 degrees for 8 hours, stirring occasionally. 2. The butter is done when there is no liquid on top of it and it has gone a deep red color. 3. Pour the butter into warm jars that have been sterilized in boiling water,

and put the lids on. 4. Seal in a boiling-water bath for 10 minutes. (For simple rules of canning, see "Bringing in the Sheaves.")

The Biscuits—Ingredients

> *2 cups all-purpose flour*
> *½ cup lard or shortening*
> *4 teaspoons baking powder*
> *1 teaspoon salt*
>
> *1 teaspoon sugar*
> *a pinch of cream of tartar*
>   *(optional)*
> *¾ cup milk*

1. Mix all the dry ingredients together in a bowl. 2. Cut in the lard or shortening and rub together with the fingertips until the mixture has the texture of fine breadcrumbs. 3. Stir in the milk, a little at a time, until the dough has combined into a ball. 4. Preheat oven to 450 degrees. 5. Turn the dough on to a floured surface and knead lightly for a few minutes; this is the trick that sets this recipe apart from all the others. The act of kneading folds air into the dough, which will then bake into an incredibly light, crumbly biscuit. 6. Roll dough out until it's a half inch thick, and cut into biscuits. 7. Bake for about 12 minutes, until biscuits turn a light golden brown.

Happy Herb-Day to Me

I T'S EARLY—SO EARLY THAT THE DOGS ARE
still asleep upstairs, draped over each other at the
foot of the bed, with noses and paws in the air. It's
early—so early that the morning is cool, its silence punctuated
only by the occasional birdcall and inquiring honks from the
geese gathered in the barn. "I'll be back later," I declare firmly,
moving on before they can protest. This June dawn is just for
me—a gift I've been promising myself since the anniversary of
my birth back in April.

I used to put so much stock in that event. My teens and twenties were spent trying to recapture the excitement of childhood, the weeks of anticipation leading up to a day that was almost as special as Christmas. But no matter how elaborate the party or how entertaining the guests, my adult celebrations were never quite the same. I had to wait until I had a child of my own before rediscovering those joys in Charley's sparkling eyes. Nowadays I like to spend my birthday very quietly with the family, taking in a movie and maybe dinner up in town. My only indulgence is a present to myself—one day in which to do something that would otherwise get pushed aside. In past years I've visited museums that interest only me; or used the time to finish a piece of furniture; or even just read a book. It doesn't really matter how the day is spent as long as it regenerates the spirit and lets me briefly enjoy being my most individual self. This year I was going to redesign my herb garden—reinvigorate the home for the plants that continuously enrich my life.

Herbs have captured my heart ever since I grew my first pot of parsley on a London windowsill. I love the delicate shapes of their leaves and the subtlety of their colors; I love all their fragrances, from the citrus tang of lemon balm to the peppery scent of basil; I love the look and taste of them in food and the pretty gifts they make; but most of all, I love what they do for my peace of mind. The simple act of garnishing a soup with homegrown chives, or flavoring a salad with freshly picked nasturtiums, can slow the crazed pace of a day down to a more natural rhythm. Suddenly I've left all those modern stresses behind and am back to more wholesome basics. It's no wonder that these humble little plants have fascinated humankind throughout history.

Herbs have been the green gold of a garden since the beginning of recorded time. The first known herbal was written by the Chinese emperor Shen Nung five thousand years ago, and the Sumerians inscribed a list of more than a thousand species on writing tablets, in 2200 B.C. Ancient Egyptian priests grew them in profusion to serve as medicine, cosmetics, or as an ingredient in the ointments with which they anointed their dead, while the Romans used them liberally in cooking. I can thank those conquerors for the wild mustard and mint that still grow in the English countryside today, because they were the ones who first brought these seeds to Britain. They planted them around their villas, not just for food but as an essential ingredient of healing tinctures and salves. The line between the curative and culinary uses of herbs wasn't really drawn until the seventeenth century and the start of the scientific age, when formal medicines began to be developed. Today, varieties are usually grown for one of four distinct purposes: culinary, cosmetic, medicinal, or household. I grow a few kinds for use in potpourris and bath salts, and one patch of pennyroyal to chase away the moths, but thirty-three of the forty-five varieties in my garden are grown, not surprisingly, for food.

It may be hard to imagine where so many herbs might fit into a normal menu, but we do use all of them, some in several different ways. For instance, cilantro (which is also known as coriander or Chinese parsley) gives us its fresh leaves for guacamole and salsa, and its lacy white blossoms to decorate our salads. The flower heads can also be water-dried (stood in a vase with about an inch of water in it, which is then allowed to evaporate) before being saved in airtight jars for use as a garnish. In the fall, we freeze the leaves to protect their delicate flavor and air-dry the seeds in their pods (which I spread out in a shallow basket and keep in a dark, dry place), to store in jars for use as one of the essential spices in Mexican and Indian meals.

The nasturtium is another multifaceted plant. A cousin of watercress, it is gifted with the same spicy taste. The leaves taste the strongest and can be used anywhere in place of its relative—in sandwiches and soups, or with fresh oranges in a salad. The blossoms are milder, but it's these that we love best. They grow in every color of the sunset, from rich golden yellow to a deep rose pink, and their velvety petals are strong enough to be stuffed with garlic cream cheese and served as a conversation-stopping appetizer. I also use them in salads and to garnish bottles of the spiced olive oil we set out on tables in the summer, as a dip for garlic bread. Occasionally, if I can summon up the self-discipline, I pick the buds before they bloom and pickle them in vinegar to make "poor man's capers." It's worth the sacrifice, because they are delicious sprinkled over smoked salmon or served with prosciutto and shaved Parmesan cheese.

Of course, not everyone has room for herbs on any scale, but I would urge even the urban apartment dweller to try growing one or two pots on a sunny window ledge. They are such sturdy plants that they will sprout despite pollution or black thumbs, and so versatile that they can reward you with all kinds of satisfaction. One of my most popular gifts, for instance, was born of some purple basil I grew on a New York fire escape. When the plants had been picked, I steeped them in white wine vinegar with a couple of heads of garlic. The resulting delicacy turned a deep rose pink and made one of the most delicious salad dressings you've ever tasted. I still make it today and often team it with another homemade vinegar, whose ingredients, before we moved to the farm, came entirely from a store: blueberry spice. They are presents that are as pretty as they are practical and both are easiness itself, yet friends seem to appreciate them more than anything we could buy.

There are so many examples of the magic that herbs can weave and I discover new tricks all the time, but perhaps their greatest gift is to capture the sunshine and give it back to us when we're buried under snow. I won't mind the work today because I know that, in the months to come, when I pluck a chili off a ristra or uncork a jar of sage, their fragrances will release the sweet memories of summer and the garden that I gave myself when I turned forty-three.

The Herbs in My Garden

Apple geranium
Basils (lemon, opal,
  cinnamon, & lettuce-leaf)
Borage

Artemisia
Bay leaves
Bee balm
Chamomile

Chives

Creeping thyme

Dill

Garlic chives

Lady's bedstraw

Lemon balm

Lemon thyme

Mints (apple, eau de cologne, chocolate, peppermint, pineapple & spearmint)

Parsley

Pennyroyal

Rosemary

Sage

Sweet woodruff

Thyme

Woolly betony

Cilantro (a.k.a. coriander, Chinese parsley)

Fennel

Heliotrope

Lavender

Lemon grass

Lemon verbena

Nasturtiums

Oregano

Paprika

Pepper (chili)

Pineapple sage

Rue

Sweet marjoram

Tarragon

Variegated sage

Some Thoughts on Preserving Herbs

There is no doubt that freezing is the best way to lock in the full flavor of herbs. The drawback is that the leaves go all mushy when they are defrosted and are useful only as a seasoning in cooking. If you want to use the herbs as a garnish, or as the ingredient for sachets and potpourri, you have to dry them. Here are some very simple tips to get you started.

The Freezing Method

This works well with all standard herbs, although personally I prefer my bay leaves, thyme, and marjoram air-dried.

Lightly wash your herbs in cool water and dry them on paper towels. When thoroughly dry, arrange on cookie sheets and place in freezer. Leave for two hours, or until deep-frozen, then gently pry off cookie sheets and store in freezer bags in serving-size portions. Label and date (don't forget to do this because they are hard to identify by sight), and store bags in an open plastic storage box on a freezer shelf.

An alternative method, which I use with chives, is to wash and dry them, then chop finely. Spoon one teaspoon of the herb into each compartment of an ice-cube tray. Fill gently with water and freeze. When frozen, turn the "ice cubes" out and store in plastic freezer bags. This method gives you your herbs preprepared and in easily measurable quantities. For soups and stews, for instance, I drop in one ice cube for each teaspoonful of herb that the recipe requires.

The Air-drying Method I

Pick off any dead or diseased leaves and trim the stems of your bunch of herbs to equal length. Rinse gently in cool water and lay out on paper towels to dry. When thoroughly dry, bind stems together with twine or a thick elastic band and hang in a dark, dry place. (I sometimes use a closet or an airing cupboard and a friend of mine keeps her herb rack in the attic. Wherever it is, it must be dry. If the air is humid, the plants will spoil.) When the herbs are dry (in about two to three weeks), take the bunches down and gently strip the leaves from the stems. Store leaves in airtight jars. (The drying bunches are very decorative, but don't be tempted to leave them hanging. The herbs will lose both taste and fragrance within days of drying if they aren't properly stored.)

The Air-drying Method II

Blossoms like bee balm and seed heads like coriander, dill, fennel, and chives cannot be hung to dry. For these I use a large basket about two inches deep that has been lined with paper towels. Clip the seed heads or the blossoms and arrange in the bottom of the basket so they aren't touching each other. Store in a dark, dry place (I lay them on top of books in our bookshelves). When dry, in about two weeks, store in airtight jars.

Stringing Ristras

We preserve many of our peppers—paprika, chili, cayenne, *jabañero,* and Hungarian—this way. They last longer and bring a splash of color to our winter kitchen. Whenever you need them for cooking, just pick the right quantity and chop, slice, or grind.

You will need a pair of rubber gloves (essential because the pepper oil can really burn your skin), a tapestry needle, and a ball of twine (I use green gardening twine; it contrasts nicely with the bright red of the peppers and makes a perfect combination when I give the ristras as Christmas presents).

Thread the needle with a long piece of twine and knot at the end. Put your rubber gloves on! Push the needle through the fleshy green cap of the pepper and pull the pepper gently down to the knot. Repeat until there are only four inches of twine left. Tie a large, secure loop in the end of the twine and hang the ristra in a sunny, dry place. In this case, the peppers thrive on light, which will bring out their full color.

Purple Basil & Garlic Vinegar

The optimum vinegar to use in this recipe is white wine vinegar, but that can be difficult to find in bulk. I often end up making it with simple distilled white vinegar, compensating for its more acidic qualities by allowing the mixture to marinate longer. The prettier the bottle this is given in, the more special the present. I save any decorative bottles I find, adding an attractive label and ribbons around its neck as the final touch.

4 cups of purple basil leaves and stems

2 large heads of garlic

1 quart white wine, or distilled white vinegar

sprigs of purple basil

1. Wash and dry basil. 2. Sterilize a glass quart storage jar in boiling water. 3. Separate cloves of garlic and remove dry, outer

skin. 4. Put dry basil and garlic in jar (water droplets can cause the vinegar to cloud). 5. Fill with vinegar to 1/2 inch from the top. 6. Gently stir using a wooden spoon and press down basil to release essential oils. 7. Screw lid on jar tightly and store in a dark cupboard for 4 to 6 weeks, until color is deep pink and fragrance of garlic and basil is very strong. 8. Strain vinegar into a bowl, then restrain through coffee filters into a jug. 9. Put a sprig of fresh basil into each sterilized decorative bottle. 10. Fill with vinegar and seal. 11. Label bottles and store in a dark cupboard.

Blueberry Spice Vinegar

This vinegar is a beautiful sapphire blue and can be used equally well as a spice or a sweetener. I use mine in salad dressings and as a syrup substitute, dribbled over fresh berries or on our breakfast pancakes.

3 pounds blueberries   *2 pints white vinegar*
4 cinnamon sticks   *white sugar*
3 whole nutmegs

1. Put vinegar and blueberries in a bowl. 2. Mash the fruit up with a potato masher and add cinnamon sticks and bruised nutmegs. 3. Cover bowl with plastic wrap. 4. Leave in a warm place for 3 days. 5. Remove spices and mash the fruit up again. 6. Strain the mixture over another bowl. 7. Repeat the process until you think that your liquid is clear. 8. Measure the juice and add 1 pound of sugar for every pint of liquid. 9. Bring mixture slowly to the boil in a thick-bottomed pan, stirring until the sugar has dissolved, then boil for 15 minutes or until the vinegar clings to the back of a teaspoon. 10. Pour into sterilized bottles and screw tops down tight. 11. Label when cool. (Makes about 3 pints.)

Ms. Manners

HEY'RE HEEERE. . . ." IT'S A JOKE THAT MY DAUGHTER has played on me before, so I ignored her and finished mopping the kitchen floor. "Mom, I'm not kidding!" she said, dragging me into the dining room so I could see the shiny Explorer being parked down by the barn. I shrieked and ran upstairs.

Greg entertained our guests while I fixed my hair and fumed about some people's lack of manners. Over the years I have learned that definitions of courtesy have many regional variations and that the well-bred Hoosier turns up right on time (as opposed to the European convention of being ten to fifteen minutes late). I'm used to that—but these guests were three-quarters of an hour early, which is inconsiderate by anybody's standards.

Miss Emily Post, that foremost arbiter of good taste, wrote about the rudeness of being tardy in her book *Etiquette,* but she didn't deal with the inconvenience caused when company arrives ahead of time. She, of course, came from a different age, when almost every one of her readers would have employed people to prepare dinner and to conduct a visitor to the drawing room, where they would be asked politely to wait. She did acknowledge the existence of the solo hostess, calling her Mrs. Three-in-One—the cook, waitress, and apparent lady of leisure—but she still expected the highest standards of organization and entertainment from her. I doubt whether Miss Post would have recognized the harassed working woman of today as she falls through the front door an hour before her dinner party starts.

I do not wish to imply that Emily Post is an anachronism. Many of this lady's fine suggestions can still be used, and she's worth reading if only to experience a gentler, more graceful era when people's primary concern was the comfort of their guests. It still should be today, I believe; but our rules of hospitality need updating if we are to be effective hosts in a modern age.

Undue punctuality is my personal bête noire and I believe the truly polite allow for everybody's pressured schedule by being ten minutes late. It is only one issue, however, in a society that is becoming increasingly complicated. Take introductions as an example. How does one introduce a couple who live together but are not married? I usually say: "This is Jim Smith and his better half (or partner in crime), Eileen Taylor." That gets a laugh, while making the point that they're together. When the couple are married, but the woman hasn't changed her name, I say: "This is Ann Rogers and her husband, Bill Jones." Easy so far— but what about a gay couple? Do they want to be acknowledged publicly as such? Even if they do, would such an acknowledgment embarrass other guests? It is the hosts' duty to make all their visitors feel at home, so this could be quite a conundrum. I solve it, British-style, by avoiding it all together: "This is Chris Black and may I introduce Keith White. . . ." The separation of the individual is also useful at business functions where one's marital status is irrelevant. I remember feeling quite insulted at a literary soiree, when I was introduced to someone simply as "Greg Murphey's wife." It made me feel as if I were defined by my husband, with no identity of my own, when in fact I had been invited there alone in my role as a writer.

Smoking is another potential minefield. Emily Post wrote pages about the subject, but in an age when smokers were in the vast majority. Today, the situation is reversed and with passions running so high on the subject, it demands some thought. I smoke cigarettes, but would never attempt to do so as a guest in a nonsmoking home. Even if I am invited to, I limit it because of the pollution it leaves behind. When nonsmokers come to us, it's more of a problem—to smoke or not to smoke becomes the question. My solution, so far, has been to indulge in the kitchen until I know the feelings of my guests—unless the weather is good, when we avoid any discomfort by eating outside. In the winters, when the house is sealed, I try to hold separate parties for the allergic or sensitive and for our smoking friends. I dread the day when I accidentally mix antismoking guests with smokers at the same table, because I'm not sure what the protocol should be. Being hospitable means considering all your guests' comfort, so at exactly what point does a hostess intervene? Maybe one answer would be to return to the old-world institution of a smoking room.

Diet is another contemporary concern. As I mentioned in "The X Factor," I always ask new visitors about their preferences, allergies, dislikes, medical restrictions etc., and tailor my menu accordingly—but it really is up to the regular guest to tell me if any of the above have changed. There is nothing worse than spending hours creating some special dish, only to see it being pushed aside. I remember one lady, who used to like "just about anything," ruining a dinner with a whole series of complaints: "I can't touch that—too much salt. . . ."; "Oh, I'm afraid I don't eat red meat anymore. . . ."; "No dessert for me, I'm watching my weight. . . ." If she'd had the courtesy to tell me all this when I invited her over, I would have happily catered to her tastes. As it was, her rudeness made everyone else feel uncomfortable and a little guilty about finishing what was on their plates.

Civility is a two-way street—dependent on the behavior of both the hosts and guests. I have, for instance, been shocked at the number of Charley's friends who have stayed with us, sometimes for days, and been entertained like little princesses, but who have then departed without saying thank you. The children aren't to blame, the parents are: they should have etched that phrase on their babies' minds from the moment they could talk. It's the rare child who learns it all alone, and yet these are two of the most important words they could use throughout their lives. I must have prompted Charley with the age-old questions ten thousand times when she was small: "What do you say . . . ?" "What's the magic word . . . ?" and so on. It was worth the effort, because courtesy, both in children and adults, makes an immediate impression. Her politeness will influence people's good opinion of her as much as her bright mind or pretty face—perhaps even more. Parents who don't teach children these rules are putting their offspring at a permanent disadvantage, because the rude child will grow into the rude adult, who finds it harder to make friends, meet the right mate, or advance in his or her career. It seems such a sin to stunt a life's potential for the sake of learning a few words.

Having said that, I must confess to not being good at the time and motion required to choose a card, buy a stamp, and get it in the mail—unless it's a special occasion. But I am good at picking up the phone, sending flowers, or writing by E-mail. As a regular hostess myself, I know how much it means to hear one's guests were pleased—and I want people who've gone to the effort of entertaining me to enjoy the same satisfaction.

Ultimately, that is the essence of good manners: to treat others the way you would wish to be treated yourself. The specifics may vary from era to era, but the basics haven't changed since human beings gathered in their first communities and were forced to find ways of keeping the peace. Good manners don't guarantee good character (some of the most ruthless people I know could charm the birds off the trees), but they do bespeak predictable behavior—that you're dealing with someone who understands the rules. This is particularly important when we share each other's food, because any animal feels at its most vulnerable when it is eating. The social graces give us a feeling of security and have enabled the act of breaking bread together to evolve beyond one that simply fuels the body, into one that enriches the soul. In Emily Post's day, nothing was left to chance; the rules for everything from clothes to conversation, table settings to the dishes served were all prescribed, allowing people to relax and enjoy within a very rigid series of parameters. In some ways, I'm glad that many of those customs have been thrown out by our more casual age, but we should be careful not to abandon them altogether. The disappearance of the little courtesies in life is one of the factors that contributes to the pressure-cooker atmosphere of the modern world. Rudeness is an attack which provokes a defense that can quickly escalate into factionalism and violence. We must never forget that the success of a social gathering—its ability to amuse, enlighten, entertain, and replenish—depends on the pleasure of everybody there and that when we choose to participate in one, we are each accepting responsibility for the happiness of all the others around the table.

Just My Cup of Tea

’M NOT SURE WHY, THE WORDS JUST SLIPPED out of my mouth and into the phone. Maybe it was the crystalline air, or the scent of the heliotropes drifting across the porch, or the alba rose blooming in its pink profusion, but I wanted to re-create the beauty of the scene and share it with a friend. No one would appreciate it more than Deborah, which is why I invited her to come for English tea.

It was only later that I winced, remembering Greg's reaction the last time I had staged such an event: he would not be pleased. My husband enjoys tea at the Ritz, or even more at the Savoy, but the preparations that go into such an occasion at home are beyond his comprehension. "Why can't you just boil a kettle and buy a cake?" he would ask grumpily, not appreciating that it's as much the manner of getting there as the end result that counts. English tea is more of a ritual than a meal, an exercise in many details that are designed to combine into one perfect moment on a sunny afternoon. Without help, it takes me about three days to get ready—which, in Greg's eyes, is a ludicrous amount of effort for what seems to be such a brief return. Perhaps you need to be born into a tea-drinking culture to understand the spiritual benefit that comes along with all that work.

I wouldn't, for instance, need to explain it to the Japanese, whose tea ceremony is even more formal than our own. Chado—the Way of Tea—is infused with the spirit of Zen Buddhism, the search to find beauty in the imperfect and symmetry in the simple acts of life. Under the guiding minds of three great tea masters—Murata Shuko, Takeno Jo-o, and Sen Rikyu—the taking of tea blossomed some five centuries ago into a complicated ceremony in which each step is governed by most specific rules. These cover everything from the way the tea is made, to the utensils used, to the flower arrangement that decorates the room, to the hut that houses it, to the very words exchanged between the host and guests. And they are all based on four principles: Wa (harmony); Kei (respect); Sei (purity); and Jyaku (tranquillity). If the first three are practiced in thought as well as deed, the masters teach, the fourth will follow. The elaborate nature of the ritual (it can take a lifetime to learn properly) is aimed at focusing both host and guest entirely on the moment so that worldly concerns will fall away and tranquillity will be achieved.

The preparation of English tea may not be rooted in any specific philosophy, but the intention behind it is very much the same: to create an experience so beautiful and balanced that it soothes and refreshes the spirit of all those who are involved.

My pleasure begins when I retrieve the china, linens, and silverware from the back of the cupboard. It's like revisiting old friends, who've been companions on and off since childhood. The cups were one of my mother's wedding gifts, made of bone china so fine that you can see the sunlight through it. I remember speaking in whispers over them as a little girl, scared that a word out of place might crack their delicate shells. I was almost equally concerned about the stiff linen tablecloth that Nana Moyce had embroidered by hand—and I would never dare to use the napkins she had edged so daintily with lace. The silver teapot belonged to my father's mother, Nana Suz, and had presided over her family gatherings for as long as I can recall.

My two grandmothers were very different women. Nana Suz didn't cook, but she was an expert hostess. She had set her early career as an opera singer aside to run the household for my grandfather, a classical musician and composer, and had gone on to entertain some of that era's best and brightest in their elegant London home. One of my most vivid childhood memories is of the foggy fall afternoons I spent at her beautifully laid table in the drawing room, eating orange sponge cakes off lace doilies and listening to her glittering conversation. My grandmother had the gift of finding exactly the right topic, pitched at exactly the right level, for whomever she was talking to, and managed to make even the five-year-old me feel like a most interesting person. Unfortunately, she never met our daughter, but Charley knows her well. The appearance of the silver teapot has always been her signal for me to tell stories about Great-grandma Suz, who made the ordinary look lovely and the lovely seem routine.

Once the silver has been polished and the linens have been starched, it's time to move on to the baking. The recipes depend on the season. In colder weather, I might make lardy cake or Bath buns—rich breads that are heavy with fruit and sugar. Their very fragrances belong to the winter and fall, filling the house with the scents of spices and warm yeast. Spring and summer, however, demand lighter fare. The British have literally hundreds of candidates to choose from and my selection usually depends on how adventurous I'm feeling. On relaxed days, when a challenge is welcome, I might make more complicated gateaux or meringues. But when time or self-confidence are in short supply, I stick to old favorites like brandy snaps, Devon splits, or Maids of Honor, and—whatever my state of mind—I always make a batch of scones. Scones are a prerequisite of English tea, served with cream and homemade jam. In Britain, the cream is "clotted"—a West Country process that turns it into a solid golden mass that stands up in the spoon. You can't buy it like that over here, but you can make a fair equivalent by beating heavy whipping cream until it separates, then draining off the whey. The remaining "curd" should be piled into a small bowl and chilled until it's time to serve. The scones are then split in two by the guest and each half is spread with the cream and one teaspoon of jam. (Strawberry is the kind most often used, but I think that raspberry or plum jam make the scones taste richer and less sweet.)

I try to finish all the baking a day ahead so I can concentrate on the sandwiches. In an English tea every detail counts and these often prosaic little snacks play a vital part in balancing the meal with a savory offering. They must, however, be as small and delicately presented as the cakes so the whole table is pleasing to the eye. I use at least two types of bread (usually whole wheat and white) to provide a contrast in texture and color. The breads are sliced very thinly, with the crusts removed, then spread with beaten sweet butter, before being shaped in a number of different ways: semisoft fillings like salmon salad or pâté with finely diced cornichons (tiny pickled gherkins) lend themselves to being rolled, chilled, then sliced crossways for a pinwheel effect; the bread can also be shaped into horns, secured with a cocktail stick, and piped full of egg and cress or a whipped garlic cream cheese; while less malleable foods like shaved ham or chicken do best when they are made into ordinary sandwiches and then cut into pretty shapes. This is how I deal with the most classic English filling of all—the cucumber.

A good cucumber sandwich is not as simple as it sounds. The cucumber must be peeled and cut thinly, but not so thin that it loses its crunch. The bread should be generously spread with butter, but not so thickly as to overwhelm the cucumber. The fill-

ing must also be seasoned with enough salt and pepper to enhance—but not engulf—the cucumber's delicate taste. Simply
put, it takes a light hand and a lot of practice!

Each type of sandwich is stored separately in the refrigerator
the night before the event so that the morning can be spent creating the scene. This is probably my favorite part of the whole
ritual, when all the individual details should finally come together into one harmonious whole. The process can't be rushed.
I have to be totally absorbed in the task to choose exactly the
right garnishes for each dish and to pick the combination of flowers and foliage that will not only enhance the table but also act as
a bridge between the formality of the setting and the natural
landscape around us. My intentions must be pure in this, because
if it looks self-conscious it won't have the right effect. Guests
can't relax if they think their hostess is showing off; they feel
under pressure to play a part in her production. But when they're
not really aware of the effort that went into the event, when they
feel simply loved and cared for, they will be at rest in their surroundings and able to enjoy one perfect moment of tranquillity
on a sunny afternoon.

An English Tea Primer

I wish there was the space here to include even a small selection of my favorite English-tea recipes, but they will have to wait for another book at a later time. There is room, however, for some very simple guidelines and for the recipes of the baked goods that I served at Deborah's tea. Let's begin with a few notes about the beverage after which this meal is named.

On Making Tea

The English have several rules about making a "good pot of tea." 1. The water should be at a full boil. 2. The pot should be "warmed" with about a half cup of boiling water, which is then discarded before the tea is made. 3. The tea should be loose and kept as fresh as possible by storage in an airtight tin or jar. 4. A measurement of one teaspoon of tea per person and one extra teaspoon for the pot should make an infusion of the right strength. 5. The tea should left to steep for at least five minutes before serving.

On Serving Tea

English tea is most usually served with cold milk and sugar. There's some acrimony in the British Isles between the MIFs (Milk In First) set and the MILs (Milk In Last). I, personally, am a MIF because I think the milk mixes better with the tea that way, but I have several friends who pour scorn on the idea, claiming that adding the milk last controls the strength of the brew. There's no right or wrong in this rather silly debate; it's a matter of personal taste. Of course many people over here don't take milk at all, so I always have a dish of lemon slices to offer as an alternative. I also set out a variety of sweeteners: natural sugar, honey, and (a discovery of ours) maple syrup. This last adds a delicious toffee undertone to the drink, which works particularly well with strong varieties of tea like Assam. And don't forget to have a pot of hot water on hand so the main teapot can be refreshed. "Teatime" in England—the hour of the day when this meal is traditionally served—is at four o'clock.

A Selection of Teas

Knowing and drinking tea is very much like knowing and drinking wine. As novice imbibers, we are perfectly happy with dusty tea bags, or bottles of supermarket red. Then, one glorious day, we are given a Formosa Oolong or a Gevrey-Chambertin to sample and life is never quite the same. Great teas, like great wines, we discover, have layer upon layer of flavors, which even vary within types according to the time picked, the grade of the leaf, and the conditions of that particular year. Selecting a tea should be an adventure where the name or ingredients on the package give only the first clues as to what the final taste might be, the rest will depend on the blend and the subtlety of the vintage.

The problem for the novice, then, is knowing where to begin. What do all those exotic names actually mean? Since there are hundreds, maybe even thousands, of alternatives to choose from, many must be discovered by personal trial and error, but I will try to help here with brief descriptions of the types of tea most often found on an English table:

• *Assam:* is one of my personal favorites because of its strong, malty flavor and a coppery-brown color that looks robust enough to revive the dead. This is the tea to serve to people in shock, or at least to friends at the end of a difficult day. The best Assam—the "first flush" or first plucking of the new leaves of the season—is a hard-to-find delicacy, but the richness of this tea's flavor remains consistent even in less expensive blends. Most "Irish Breakfast" teas are made with Assam, while "English

Breakfast" is usually Assam softened with a mix of golden Ceylon teas.

• *Darjeeling:* from the foothills of the Himalayas, is as delicate as Assam is strong. The leaves produce tea of a light honey color and a fragrant, flowery taste. First-flush Darjeelings are one of the most expensive teas in the world and are so sought after that they often don't make it to our shores. The few that do are worth the price for a taste that seems to contain within it all the blossoms of a tropical spring.

• *Formosa Oolong:* The United Kingdom Tea Council calls Darjeeling the "champagne of teas," but I'm more inclined to agree with James Norwood Pratt—author of the delightful *Tea Lover's Treasury*—who gives that distinction to Formosa Oolong. The black dragon of the beautiful isle needs no milk, sugar, or even lemon. Nothing should be allowed to interfere with this most mellow of leaves and its flavor of sun-ripened peaches.

• *Lapsang Souchong:* comes from north Fujian in China, where they dry the leaves over pinewood fires. This makes the tea taste like liquid smoke—which does not appeal to everybody. Personally, I think it's the perfect refreshment for a hot humid day, sweetened with a little honey.

• *Orange Pekoe:* is not a type of tea, it's a method of grading the tea leaf that is used in Sri Lanka. The grade of the leaf has no bearing on its flavor, but most blends sold as Orange Pekoe can be assumed to be Ceylon tea, a golden drink that tastes as bright and brisk as its color would suggest.

• *Earl Grey:* is a blended tea which now has such a variety of recipes attached to its name that its purchase is no longer any guarantee of content or quality. The original blend, named after an eighteenth-century British aristocrat who once served as an envoy to China, was supposedly a mix of Chinese and Indian black teas, flavored with oil of bergamot, a citrus fruit. This last ingredient is probably the only common denominator in today's concoctions, which are sometimes so drenched in the oil that the beverage tastes bitter. But when the bergamot is applied in moderation, it gives this light tea its distinctive and delicate perfume. Earl Grey is usually taken black, but can be drunk with a little cloud of milk.

English Scones

There are as many ways of making scones as there are of making biscuits, including some that add raisins to the mix. These fruit breads are delicious when buttered, but they don't go well with cream and jam. I've made my scones the same way since I was a little girl, when my mum taught me the following recipe:

1¾ cups all-purpose flour   *½ stick of butter*
1 pinch of salt   *½ teaspoon baking soda*
1 teaspoon cream of tartar   *½ cup milk*
beaten egg

1. Preheat the oven to 450 degrees. 2. Sift all the dry ingredients together into a bowl. 3. Rub the butter in with the fingertips until the mix looks like coarse breadcrumbs. 4. Add the milk slowly until you have a soft, pliable dough. 5. Turn the dough out onto a floured surface and knead for a few minutes. 6. Roll out the dough to about half an inch thick and cut out the scones with a fluted 2-inch cookie cutter. 7. Let the scones relax for a minute while you grease a baking tray. 8 Set the scones on the tray at least half an inch apart from each other. 9. Brush their tops with

a little of the beaten egg. 10. Bake for about 10 minutes, until they're golden brown.

Devon Splits

In Britain, English teas are sometimes called "cream teas," particularly in the West Country, where this rich food is produced in such abundance. Devonshire cream is the most famous kind of all and this sweet bun is designed to hold as much of it as possible!

3½ cups all-purpose flour	*1 package yeast*
1 cup warm water	*1 egg*
a pinch of salt	*6 tablespoons sugar*
¼ cup butter	*½ cup raspberry jam*
½ pint heavy whipping cream	*1 capful vanilla*
confectioners' sugar	

1. Beat the egg. 2. Soften the yeast with the warm water and stir in 1 teaspoon of the sugar, the egg, and 4 tablespoons of the flour. 3. Cover and set aside in a warm place for a half hour. 4. In

the meantime sift the rest of the flour, sugar, and the salt into a large mixing bowl. 5. When the yeast has finished working, fold into the flour mixture, combining thoroughly. 6. Knead in the butter and keep kneading until the dough is smooth. 7. Grease a bowl and put the dough in it. 8. Cover and leave it to rise in a warm place for 30–40 minutes. 9. Turn the dough out onto a floured surface and roll out lightly. 10. Divide it into 20 pieces and shape each piece into a ball. 11. Let the dough rest for a few minutes before rolling out each ball again into flattened circles about 3 inches wide. 12. Fold the circles in half, but do not press together. 13. Grease a baking sheet with butter and arrange the circles on it, at least a half inch apart. 14. Set the buns aside in a warm place again to rise, for another 45 minutes. 15. Preheat the oven to 425 degrees. 16. Bake the buns for about 10 minutes, until they're golden brown. 17. Turn them out onto a wire rack and leave to cool. 18. Whip the cream with the vanilla until it is stiff. 19. Warm the jam until it's liquid, then pass it through a sieve into a bowl, which should be set aside to cool. 20. When the buns are cold, pull them apart gently and fill the centers with the whipped cream and the jam. 21. Lay the buns out on a board and lightly dust them with sifted confectioners' sugar.

Brandy Snaps

These delicious wafers are also full of cream and are particularly popular in the northern part of Britain. The basic recipe below was given to me by a Gypsy lady whose caravan always had the longest lines waiting to buy her brandy snaps at the Humberside Fall Fair. Over time I added the grated orange peel and a little extra ginger. If golden syrup is difficult to find, a mixture of corn and maple syrup may be substituted:

7 tablespoons all-purpose flour
¼ cup sugar
1 teaspoon ground ginger
  (fresh, if possible)
½ pint heavy whipping cream
½ teaspoon of orange or
  ginger essence (optional)

¼ cup butter
2 tablespoons golden syrup
grated rind of ½ an orange
1 tablespoon soft brown sugar

1. Preheat the oven to 350 degrees. 2. Thoroughly grease 2 baking sheets and the handle of a large wooden spoon. 3. Melt the butter, sugar, and syrup over a low heat, stirring continuously. 4. Sift the flour and ginger together, then pour in the syrup

mix, stirring as you go. 5. Stir in the orange rind. 6. Using a greased teaspoon, drop a spoonful of the mixture at intervals of 3 to 4 inches on the baking sheets. 7. Put one of the sheets in the top half of the oven and watch it carefully. This mix burns easily! The wafers are done when they are a bubbling golden brown. It usually takes 8–10 minutes. 8. Take the sheet out of the oven and remove a wafer. Put the sheet back at the bottom of the oven. 9. Quickly roll the wafer loosely around the greased spoon handle. 10. Let it set slightly, then slip it off on to a cooling rack. 11. Re-grease the spoon handle and repeat the process. 12. Obviously, timing is everything here, so I try to stagger the rate at which the wafers bake by turning the sheet often. 13. When the wafers are cool, store them in an airtight box until it's time to serve. 14. Just before tea, whip the cream, brown sugar, and one of the flavorings, if desired, until the cream is stiff. 15. Either pipe the cream or spoon it into the opposite ends of each snap. 16. Serve the snaps immediately. This recipe makes about 16 of them.

Maids of Honor

No tea would be complete without some kind of tart. This is one of my favorites because the filling is so quintessentially English. Legend has it that the recipe was first invented for the ladies-in-waiting of Henry VII's court:

For the dough:
1 cup of all-purpose flour	1 tablespoon shortening
3 tablespoons butter	2 tablespoons chilled water

For the filling:
⅓ cup superfine sugar	1 egg
½ cup ground almonds	1 lemon
1 tablespoon heavy cream	4 teaspoons raspberry jam
3 tablespoons softened butter	

1. Set aside 3 tablespoons of the flour. 2. Sieve the rest into a bowl and rub in the fats until the mixture has the texture of coarse breadcrumbs. 3. Add the water a little at a time until you have achieved a smooth dough. 4. Roll the dough out lightly on a floured board, then wrap in plastic wrap and chill in the refrig-

erator for at least 1 hour. 5. Grate the rind of the lemon. 6. Preheat the oven to 375 degrees. 7. Grease a tartlet tin. 8. Roll out the dough again and cut into twelve 2 1/2-inch rounds. 9. Line the tin with the rounds. 10. Cream the butter and sugar together. 11. Beat the egg and add to the butter mixture. 12. Stir in the almonds, lemon rind, and cream. 13. Cover the bottom of each tart with jam. 14. Fill the tarts 2/3 full with the creamy filling. 15. Bake for about 15 minutes, until the tops of the tarts are a light golden brown.

Tipping the Scales

T LOOKED OMINOUS FROM THE MOMENT I GOT ON AND the dial started spinning at supersonic speed. It slowed at the 140 mark, the needle swinging indecisively between 143 and 145. Oh dear! I sighed and went to get the size-twelve summer wardrobe out. Sometimes writing can be bad for my health. I needed to leave the keyboard more often and get some exercise.

There was a time when that would not have been my solution, a time when I managed my weight by eating once every three days. I even got scurvy at college by spending one semester trying to survive on cups of coffee! I was only partially successful at best—weighing 123 pounds at my skinniest and turning my body into a ravenous machine that could find fat in a piece of cucumber. This silly state of affairs continued until I met Greg, who persuaded me that it wasn't a healthy way to live. "Look at me," he'd say, showing off his ultraslim figure, "I stay like this by eating sensibly." His idea of "sensible" was three heavy meals daily, which he insisted that I share. In our first year together, I ballooned from a size nine up to a size twelve and would have kept on going if I hadn't found the courage to protest. People are born with different metabolisms, I pointed out, and mine just couldn't handle the calories that he needed. "Okay . . ." he admitted grudgingly, "but no more starving yourself—and no more trying to be someone you're not." He was right, of course. At my healthiest best (when I feel good, look reasonable, and don't see-saw around), I weigh about 133 pounds. That has been true since I was twenty and it was time for me to accept the way that I'd been made. Truly attractive women, Greg contends, don't have to be classic beauties, but they must have that inner light that comes from being happy with who they really are.

I wish I could bottle my husband and distribute him nation-wide; just think of the suffering he could alleviate. We've become a nation plagued by eating disorders, a people who approach food not as a blessing but as an enemy or an addictive drug. I don't know whom I feel sorrier for: the shut-in consuming twelve thousand calories a day in a fruitless attempt to satisfy some other kind of hunger, or the woman who lives in a constant state of semistarvation just so she can squeeze herself into a size four. They are both victims of an age where people believe that their happiness depends on "fitting in" and that they have been—or could be—found wanting. The experts tell us that many of the chronically obese started out as "just a little heavy," but then retreated behind fortified walls of flesh when they felt rejected. While the ladies who spend their lives counting the fat grams in each *pomodoro* are just as insecure, trapped in a Dorian Gray nightmare where the only successful women are young, thin, and suntanned—a fashion that was once the stereotype of the working poor. It's supposed to be a healthy image, too—but how long would that last, I wonder, if the great designers decided that the prosperous curves and pale skin of Victorian times were the latest definition of desirable? Feeling well and looking good are perfectly reasonable aims, but we really must stop going to extremes.

If nothing else, consider the message we're sending to our children: that beauty is only skin-deep and that successful people all look the same. It's a recipe for disaster, which, at best, will produce adults that see the world in a very one-dimensional way and, at worst, sets many of these kids up for automatic failure. Why can't we teach them to appreciate the beauty and wisdom that can shine from an older face, or about the loveliness of the models in paintings by Renoir? Why don't we concentrate their attention more on the evils of selfishness, prejudice, cruelty, even skin cancer, rather than focusing their young minds on the importance of image? Greg and I do try with Charley—particularly recently, since she's made friends with a ten-year-old who is suffering from the early signs of anorexia. The child is obsessed with what everyone weighs and we worry about our daughter succumbing to peer pressure. Not that Charley's heavy. In fact, she's a very pretty girl who is complimented regularly by strangers— which is something else she has had to learn to keep in perspective. Life, we tell her, should be a continual search for the right balance between work and play; time and money; instinct and experience; doing and listening; desire and need . . . the list goes on and on. We don't expect her to grasp it all at once—her parents haven't yet. . . . We just hope that she'll be able to head into the world with some real understanding of what makes her well and happy.

Being perceptive about himself is a great gift of Greg's, one that may have helped him more than any other. It explains, for instance, how he's managed to put on only five pounds since he was at college twenty-two years ago, despite his love of cooking and consuming good food. He listens to his body, not simply to its level of hunger but to its specific needs. He has taught me to listen, too, and I've discovered that, when left to its own devices, a body is a self-regulating organism that prefers to eat seasonally. In the spring, for instance, our taste for meat begins to disappear, to be replaced by an overwhelming desire for fresh greens. By the summer, we turn semivegetarian, happily surviving on light meals of pasta, salad, vegetables, and fruit—with some chicken or fish. Our appetite for salt also goes way up, presumably because we need to replace what we've lost in perspiration, while my taste for sodas, diet or otherwise, evaporates and I spend the warmer months drinking gallons of ice water. It may sound very commendable, but we're not following any rules. If we want a steak, we'll have one—and I've noticed that I do crave red meat about once a month, when I need the extra iron.

We take the same approach to "forbidden" foods like eggs or butter: if you truly hunger for them, your body is trying to tell you something. Recent medical research has confirmed what my husband has always sensed—that an unduly low cholesterol count can be as dangerous as one that's too high and that every diet needs a little salt, sugar, and fat.

Simply put, we try to approach eating in the same way we approach life: with a sense of moderation—and with gratitude, too. Being in the country has reminded us that our sustenance is always another living thing's loss, even if it's at second or third hand. Whether it's a fish, or a lettuce, or a piece of shrink-wrapped beef, some cycle was cut short to satisfy our hunger. The only fit way to honor these sacrifices is truly to appreciate our food and to be thankful for the gifts we're given each day on our plates.

Summer Pleasures

Frosted peach fizz, fresh tomatoes and basil, corn cooked the moment after it's picked, are just a few of the many tastes that speak of summer days. Most of our favorites don't need a recipe (we try not to dribble away our lovely days in the kitchen), and even those that do are extremely easy to make:

Sevice

This sumptuous fish salad came originally from Peru, but I got the recipe from my friend Linsey Powers. It will serve six as an appetizer for dinner or it can used as a dip for a party.

4 cups scallops, tuna, or any firm-fleshed fish	1 small bunch fresh parsley
1 green pepper, finely chopped	½ cup lemon juice
1 clove garlic, minced	1 red pepper, finely chopped
2 teapoons chili powder	2 teaspoons minced fresh ginger
¼ teaspoon fresh ground black pepper	¼ teaspoon cayenne-pepper flakes
	½ teaspoon salt

1. Cut the fish into thin strips. 2. Rinse in cold water and pat dry on paper towels. 3. Put into a bowl and mix in all the other ingredients, thoroughly coating the fish. 4. Marinate for 8 hours in the refrigerator. 5. Garnish with tiny snips of fresh parsley before serving.

Barbecued Salmon

Four years ago we decided to dispense with our annual July mega-party and have just a small gathering of friends instead. We also decided to abandon the traditional hamburgers, bratwurst, and hot dogs on the grill for one whole barbecued salmon. Our changes were such a success that we've been celebrating Independence Day this way ever since, with the same group of people and the same menu.

one 5–7 pound fresh whole salmon (have the head removed and the fish cleaned)	*seasoned salt*
	finely ground white pepper
	1 stick of butter, softened
4 limes	*Olive oil or butter*

1. Heat the coals in the barbecue. 2. When hot, spread them around the sides to cook indirectly. 3. Set an aluminum-foil drip pan in the center of the coals. 4. Grease a large piece of heavy-duty aluminum foil with either olive oil or butter. 5. Squeeze the juice from the limes into a cup or jug. 6. Place the fish on the foil and sprinkle both the inside and out liberally with the lime juice. 7. Spread the softened butter on the inside and outside of the

salmon. 8. Season lightly with the salt and pepper. 9. Fold the foil around the fish and seal the edges. 10. Place the foil package on the barbecue grill, cover, and cook for approximately 1 hour. Don't forget to check the coals and add to them if necessary. 11. Remove the fish from the heat. Unwrap the foil and remove the skin of the fish (this should pull away easily). 12. Serve on a platter with tartar sauce and lime wedges on the side.

Coeur à la crème

Since our summer appetizers and main courses are so simple, I like to take a little more trouble over our desserts. This French classic makes a delightful centerpiece, particularly if it is edged with the leaves from whichever berries you are using. I prefer gooseberries because their tartness is a nice contrast to the sweetness of the cream. They also have the prettiest heart-shaped leaves.

1 8-ounce tub cream cheese
(full fat)
1 tablespoon white sugar

2 egg whites
½ pint whipping cream
½ teaspoon vanilla

1. Press the cream cheese into a mixing bowl through a sieve, using a wooden spoon. 2. Beat in whipping cream with an egg whisk or electric beater until smooth. 3. Stir in sugar and vanilla. 4. Beat egg whites until stiff and fold into mixture. 5. Pour into heart-shaped mold. 6. Leave overnight in the refrigerator to drain. 7. Unmold immediately before serving and either serve with fresh berries or with berry sauce (see next recipe).

Gooseberry Sauce

*2 cups fresh gooseberries
    (best if hand-picked
    when rose-colored)
½ cup of sugar
⅓ cup water*

*2 tablespoons half-and-half
½ teaspoon lemon juice
2 teaspoons cornstarch
nutmeg*

1. Top and tail the gooseberries and wash. 2. Warm the berries in a pan with water, lemon juice, sugar, and 1 tablespoon of half-and-half. 3. Cook over slow heat until berries are soft and popping. 4. Strain through a sieve over a mixing bowl, pushing the

meat of the berries through with a wooden spoon and discarding the skins. 5. Return the berry mixture to a clean pan and gently warm. 6. Beat in cornstarch and remaining half-and-half, seasoning with nutmeg to taste. 7. Serve chilled, garnished with gooseberry leaves and fresh berries.

Bringing in the Sheaves

HE GARDEN LOOKED BLASTED . . . WEEDY . . . bereft . . . like a neglected child crying for attention. The sight of it saddened me so much that I had spent the most beautiful days of the year skulking inside. We'd made our decision not to plant that spring, when travel and work schedules were threatening to overwhelm us. It had seemed sensible, even desirable, at the time, but I'd felt thrown off course all summer, and as the weather began to cool I bitterly regretted it.

The peach-colored days that see August into September are

made for us to harvest. We are supposed to get up early and pluck the beans that dangle plumply from the vine, while the catbird sings its paean to the beginning of the day. We are meant to enjoy the misty air as we collect the first windfall of apples from the orchard and trudge them back to the house in big baskets. It is right for us to mourn the cilantro, cucumbers, and zucchini as they say their good-byes, easing our sense of loss when they set seed for the next season. A harvest, I realized too late, means completion, continuity, a renewal of hope. It's one of the few times in life when hard work guarantees some kind of rich reward.

In normal years I'm too busy to think such poetic thoughts, as food is piled throughout the house requiring my immediate attention. There are peppers screaming to be strung; herbs demanding to be dried; red cabbages begging to be chopped and cooked with their apple counterparts. But they all have to wait until we've dealt with my husband's huge crop of tomatoes. At harvesttime, I begin to believe that Greg grows all his different varieties deliberately to torture me. I don't feel this way when he shyly produces the first lush Early Girls for us to taste, or covers a dinner plate with one thick slice from a Brandywine—but when I'm faced with buckets full of Abraham Lincolns, Mortgage Lifters, and 1884s, I get a little testy. And when he adds the Romas, San Marzanos, and the Principe Borghese to the piles, I'm almost ready to quit. The problem—and the delight—is that they are all utterly distinct from one another, both in terms of taste, looks, and the functions that they serve. Some make wonderful salsa, or the perfect paste, or a sumptuous marinara sauce. The Principe Borghese are scrumptious sun-dried, while we prefer to freeze the Mortgage Lifters whole to seal in their rich flavor. Each recipe is its own mini-marathon and it can take days to put up the whole crop. People often ask us why we bother, then they taste our chutney or arrabiata sauce and begin to understand. Even the best of the best store-bought fruits only faintly echo the depth of Greg's tomatoes.

This isn't true of all supermarket produce. In an effort to recapture some of that September's magic, I plundered our local grocery for the ingredients to make our much-loved golden pickles. It was a good time to buy—summer squash, onions, cauliflower, even carrots, were at their cheapest and they cooked up into the same glorious sweet-and-sour relish that we usually make straight from the garden. Even in seasons when we have a full harvest of our own, we keep an eye out for bargains in the stores that can be turned into some of the family's favorite delicacies. We may not be able to grow our own lemons, olives, or tropical fruit, but we can still enjoy lemon curd, tapenade (the spicy olive-and-anchovy paste from the south of France), or candied kumquats, for only pennies per jar. Our friends can, too, in the Christmas baskets that we give them. They ooh and ah over these treats as if there were something miraculous about them, refusing to listen when I say how easy canning and preserving can be. The truth is that you don't require a lot of space or tools, or any specialized skill—all you need is a stove, some lids, jars, and a large saucepan, to begin what is one of the most rewarding ways of spending time in the kitchen.

The greatest pleasure for me, however, lies in seeing the whole process through from start to finish. No matter how often I do it, I can never quite believe that the twelve small seeds I planted in June grew to produce the fifty or sixty dark green zucchinis I'm freezing in September. And when we bring them out again in the winter to make *ratatouille* with our other stores, it feels as if we're fulfilling a fundamental human need: to provide food for our children that depends on nothing more than our ability and willingness to work with nature. That may sound unnecessary, even anachronistic, in this modern age—but to us, it counterbalances the helplessness we all experience occasionally in the face of a science and a society that are increasingly hard to understand. When the computer crashes or the car won't start, or Greg is having trouble with a client, it's a comfort to know that the production of our food, at least, is still under our control. There's a sense of safety and freedom in a full freezer and shelves of shining jars, a peace of mind that we once denied ourselves for an entire season.

Needless to say, we didn't starve that winter and our friends survived their store-bought gifts, but we'll never do it again. We've discovered that a little of our happiness depends on being part of the seasonal cycle, and no matter how busy we get, we must make the time to plant some kind of garden. It may be an acre or just a patch by the back door, but we need the promise of the seeds as they sink into the earth and the small triumph of watching the new sprouts emerge. When we're swamped with work, it does us good to be drawn outside to feel the sun on our hair while we weed and water, serenaded by the bees as they busily pollinate our plants. And nothing is more satisfying to the human spirit than seeing it all come to fruition when we spend a few mellow days, each fall, bringing in the sheaves.

Some Thoughts on Canning & Preserving

The basic rule is clean, clean, and clean again. Bacteria is what makes food rot, so every lid, seal, and jar should be sterilized in boiling water before you begin. If you're preserving in bulk, it is worth steaming all the equipment in a boiling water bath for ten minutes, or running it all through the dishwasher. For small batches, I simply half fill the jars with water and put them in the microwave for the same length of time. I clean the lids and seals by soaking them in a bowl of boiling water.

The second-most important rule is to make sure that the jars are sealed. Let the jars cool on towels or a wooden board. (Never put hot jars on a cold counter, they might crack.) As the vacuum forms under each lid you will hear a ping sound. When the jars are cold, test the lids by pushing down on the center of each. If the lids are solid, without any give, they are properly sealed. If they make a clicking sound, like those little metal frogs that children play with, something has gone wrong. The jar should be refrigerated and its contents eaten immediately.

Finally, label all your preserves and store them in a cool, dark cupboard where sunlight cannot get to them.

Golden Pickles

This spicy-sweet family favorite was first made for us by our dear friend Jacque Schultze. I begged her for the recipe and it has since become one of the most popular items in our Christmas gift baskets. They are delicious, easy to make, and the ingredients are available at most supermarkets throughout the year:

1 gallon sliced summer
  squash and zucchini
2 heads cauliflower
2 carrots
1 red pepper
5 cups sugar
2 tablespoons mustard seed

1 tablespoon turmeric
⅓ cup salt
6 onions
3 green peppers
3 cloves garlic
3 cups white vinegar
1½ teaspoons celery seed

1. Clean and chop the vegetables. 2. Soak them all for 3 hours in water and ice. 3. Drain them thoroughly. 4. Warm the vinegar. 5. Stir in the sugar, mustard seed, celery seed, and turmeric. 6. Keep stirring until the sugar has dissolved and the mixture has become syrupy. 7. Pour the syrup over the drained vegetables. 8. Bring them to a boil in an earthenware pot (do not use a metal

one). 9. Pour into warm jars that have been sterilized in boiling water. 10. Put the lids on and seal in a boiling-water bath for 10 minutes.

Lemon Curd

I've already given this secret away in my first book, *Bean Blossom Dreams,* but it is such a much-loved gift that I think it's worth repeating here. It makes a wonderful filling for tarts, or reheated as a lemon sauce for sponge cake, or simply spread on buttered toast. This recipe makes four 8-ounce jars.

3 lemons	*3 eggs, well-beaten*
1 stick salted butter	*1¼ cups superfine sugar*

1. Rub whole lemons against a small-tooth grater to remove the yellow part of the peel. (Try to avoid the white pith, it tastes bitter.) 2. Set the grated peel aside and cut the lemons in half. 3. Squeeze their juice into a small bowl and remove any stray lemon pits. 4. Place the butter and sugar in the top half of a dou-

ble boiler with simmering water in the lower part. (If you don't have a double boiler, use a basin over a pan of water.) 5. Stir well until the butter has melted. 6. Stir the grated rind and the juice from the lemons into the melted butter. 7. Stir in the eggs. 8. Keep stirring the mix over the simmering water as the curd thickens, which takes about 20–25 minutes. 9. Remove it from the heat and pour it into the warm, sterilized jars. 10. Put the lids on immediately and screw them down tight. 11. Label them when the jars are cold and store in the refrigerator, where the curd will keep for about 9 weeks.

Tomato Salsa

No matter how many jars I make of this, it always seems to disappear—so be warned! People particularly like it at Christmas when its garden-fresh ingredients and rich tomato-y taste bring back happy memories of summer.

4 cups chopped tomato
½ cup finely chopped onion

1 cup seeded and finely chopped
sweet red pepper

2 cups seeded and chopped
banana pepper, jalapeño
pepper, or a mix of both.
(Adjust according to your
preferred level of heat.)
1 cup seeded and finely chopped
sweet green pepper

3 heaped tsps. minced garlic
⅓ cup chopped fresh cilantro
1½ teaspoons salt
½ teaspoon brown sugar
½ cup distilled white vinegar

1. Sterilize 6 half-pint jars in a boiling-water bath. 2. Combine all the ingredients together in a saucepan and bring to the boil. 3. Reduce the heat to low and simmer, stirring occasionally, for 1 hour. 4. Pour the salsa into the warm jars, leaving about 1/2 inch of headspace at the top of each. 5. Screw the lids on and process in a boiling-water bath for 30 minutes.

Dreams . . .

HE TV SHOW WANTED TO COME DOWN AND see us cook. "Can't we come to the studio?" I asked tentatively. "Or perhaps we could film it on location elsewhere." The producer sounded puzzled until I explained that we work out of a tiny, undesigned galley kitchen with barely room for one chef—let alone two and an entire crew. "We've been through this before," I went on apologetically. "You can only shoot one angle of an area that doesn't even have a rustic kind of charm." Finally, she invited us up to the studio instead and spared us the ordeal of trying to camouflage what is, in truth, a really ugly space.

Normally, we don't think of it as such. Kitchens, for both Greg and me, fall into two categories: the gleaming architectural wonders that we admire in the pages of glossy magazines; and the ill-equipped, awkward realities that we've had to adapt to all our lives. Our pasts are full of stories about dinner cooked for twelve on two burners and a chopping board, so the small inconveniences don't faze us much at all. That is, until we're forced to see them through someone else's eyes. Then we wonder whether we should plunge in and make a few improvements, instead of waiting until we can do everything at once. But we both share the unspoken superstition that impatience now might provoke the fates and eventually cost us the kitchen of our dreams.

"The Kitchen of Our Dreams" is an ongoing discussion that has entertained us for years. It's a free-falling fantasy, escapism without penalty or price. It doesn't even lead to arguments, because although we differ on some details, Greg and I usually agree about the big things in life. We have both, for instance, imagined taking the back off the house and building a sunny, multipurpose space for the whole family to enjoy. It would be nice be able to cook—together—while Charley paints pictures in the crafts area, or reads a book stretched out on a big, comfy couch. We'd like a fireplace in front of that couch and a media center so we could all listen to music or watch a movie while we worked. When we entertain guests, we'd prefer it if they could talk to us at their ease, instead of perched on a stool in the corner, addressing the backs of our heads. There'd be a dining area for them, of course, in front of French windows that open onto the kitchen garden so produce could be taken directly from the earth, as and when required. In the winters, we'd still pick fresh herbs and greens from a hydroponic unit set somewhere to the side—probably near the door to the root cellar or the walk-in pantry. And, at the center of it all, there would be a state-of-the-art, mother-eat-your-heart-out, drop-dead-gorgeous kitchen.

This is where our fantasy starts to get expensive. Since money is no object, we'd pick out at least one and sometimes two of the best of everything. We'd want his and her ranges, for instance, to accommodate our different styles. Greg would choose an authentic Japanese hibachi grill with four electric burners on the side, set into a large U-shaped island from where he could cook, converse, and control the social flow. While mine would be a six-burner gas range set into the countertop along the wall, between a built-in (but removable) marble slab for pastry and a large butcher's block. This is where I could work unobserved, losing myself in the preparation of sauces and hors d'oeuvres, or in the delicate precision of elaborate desserts.

The two areas would be a reflection of who we are and how we dovetail together both as cooks and as a couple. Our dinner parties always work best when I orchestrate the overture and the finale in the background, while Greg steps forward to conduct the main event.

As a matter of curiosity, I recently asked a dear friend and talented architect, Jonathan Hess, to put a price tag on our fantasy. He sat back and began adding up out loud, listing interesting but scary options like a convection/micro/thermal oven and solid beech cabinets with stainless steel tops. Throw in a designer dishwasher . . . fridge-freezer . . . recessed lighting . . . and we were looking at about . . . ummm . . . 150,000 bucks. . . . Allow me to spell that out: one hundred and fifty thousand dollars for a kitchen that would be worth more than our entire house! That's a bit rich—even for a dream. And when I think about it seriously, I'm not sure that the return would justify the investment.

A new kitchen wouldn't make us better cooks, for instance. That talent comes from within and will exercise itself with the simplest of tools. Greg works such wonders with a wok and a skillet that a hibachi grill would just give him another way to fry. While I already own a marble slab, not built-in but portable, which allows me to convert our one countertop into a baking area that copes with almost everything I make. During the holidays, when Charley and I are having one of our marathon cookie sessions, we simply spill out onto the dining table only steps away. Our dream would mean more space, certainly, but we don't normally cook for more than six and don't need a setup that could cater for an army. In fact, if I'm honest, I must admit that our home as it is now works well and satisfies almost every requirement on our fantasy list.

We have gardens growing right by the back door and can even cut herbs in winter from the little hydroponic unit in the sunroom off our kitchen. On many evenings, this is where Charley paints her pictures while Greg or I are cooking dinner. The open-plan design of our dear old farmhouse (where the rooms all flow into each other to circulate the air), ensures that we're always within talking and listening distance, whatever we're up to individually. It also gives us the perfect space for keeping stores—in the old well house where it stays cool through the worst Hoosier heat. The only two things the layout won't allow us to do is cook together, or accommodate film crews comfortably in the kitchen. Even if we had $150,000 lying around, my conscience wouldn't let me spend it on such trivial concerns.

In any case, as Jonathan went on to point out, a real home should be like a second skin: snug, a good fit, a true expression of ourselves. Yes, we can smooth out a few wrinkles—but we must be careful not to clean up its character lines instead. We love the way the traffic flows through and around the house, and the way the whole space always seems alive. A new addition would centralize all that activity, leaving entire rooms plunged into darkness. We might not like that. Some changes should be grown into gradually to avoid mistakes along the way.

This is clearly how the great Julia Child approached her kitchen, if a picture I saw the other day is anything to go by. It was a delightful higgledy-piggledy collection of unmatched cabinets, older appliances, and well-used pans festooned across the walls. It wasn't a showroom or a museum, it was a place where someone cooked and had cooked for a lifetime, creating a thousand offerings for her fortunate family and friends. It was a wonderful space which glowed with a generosity and promise of good food that no architect, however brilliant, could create. It was the kitchen I've always wanted—it is the kitchen we already have—with one notable difference. Ms. Child's centers around a large table, bleached blond by the scrubbing of the years. It looked like the perfect place for a second cook to work, or for guests to sit at while she's serving dinner. A slightly smaller model would be the answer for us and all we'd have to do is take down one plywood wall. Life is good when we can make dreams come true for a coat of paint and a couple of hundred dollars. . . .

We Are What We Eat

'M HUNGRY!" MY DAUGHTER'S DECLARATION was no surprise: it usually surfaces between "how did it go?" and "have you got any homework?" It is part of the daily litany when we pick her up from school and we have learned to be ready for her. I handed over a granola bar and a bunch of grapes. "Oh . . . thank you," Charley said, trying to sound grateful as she gazed longingly at the lines of cars waiting at the drive-thrus. There was a time when we would have been there with them, a brief era when we'd stop almost every day. Then we woke up to our laziness and made a new rule: four nutritious snacks for every fried meal. It wasn't our most popular decision, but even a nine-year-old won't claim that a constant stream of hamburgers is healthy. She knows they're not good for her body, but she's a little young to understand yet that too much fast food can also be bad for society in general.

I don't want to give the impression that I'm a lackey for the Food Police—far from it. I'm sick of their dramatic announcements about the poisons they keep finding in all our favorite treats. They seem to think that we should exist on a diet of ice water and lettuce leaves—not giving our bodies the credit for being the complex organisms they are. I would like them to explain why an old-time frontiersman could live to the age of ninety on ten pounds of buffalo meat and a bottle of whiskey each day, while the nonsmoking, nondrinking, healthy go-getter suddenly leaves us at the age of forty-five. Most people stay in reasonable shape by taking their pleasures sensibly. The others might concentrate less on what's in their food and more on what mines lie waiting for them in their family genes.

Nor am I against snacks, per se. We've been eating on the run ever since cavemen carried a pouch full of dried meat and berries to avoid the inconvenience of having to stop for lunch midway through the chase. But that wasn't their consistent diet. When the hunt was over or the gathering was done, our ancestors would celebrate with a feast of the best food they could muster. Throughout history, eating well has been a point of pride—a symbol of our power, culture, wealth, of our very humanity. It's an ancient equation: the more various the foods and seasonings available, the more civilized and prosperous we deem ourselves to be. Even Puritan America approved of a bountiful table, provided it didn't lead to gluttony or greed. Our forefathers wolfed down meals of roast beef, chicken, and oyster stifle, wild turkey, clam chowder, potatoes, succotash, corn bread, and an assortment of pies and pandowdies, with a clear conscience. The Bible itself had taught them that these were gifts from God: "Every moving thing that liveth may be meat for you, even as the green herb have I given you all things" (Genesis 9:3). And they knew that they were expected to appreciate these gifts: "For every creation of God is good, and nothing to be refused, if it be received with thanksgiving." (I Timothy 4:4). Food, the Scriptures made clear, was not just to be treated as sustenance but as a celebration of the Lord's covenant with humankind. In recent times food may have been regarded more as a testament to America's abundance and diversity, or to the culture's increasing sophistication, but it has always been seen as a blessing—which is what makes our growing dependence on those drive-thrus so disturbing.

Mass-produced patties on blotting-paper buns are not food in this context. They are simply fuel: anonymous calories that taste and look the same whether we're eating them in Moscow, Minneapolis, or at any point in between. They do not enrich, elevate, or celebrate any tradition. They satisfy nothing more than the basest hunger at the fastest possible speed. This product is designed to be efficient and to keep us efficient, too—boosting our flagging energy enough to get us back on the move. I see little difference between it and the fodder we feed to our barn animals—which may explain why eating at a fast food restaurant can sometimes feel like being slopped at a trough. That's not good for the human spirit. It robs us of our individuality in tiny increments, until we seem as faceless and interchangeable as polystyrene plates.

Some argue that this is quite deliberate—that we are being prepared for an overpopulated world where the majority will be drones—but I don't think it's that calculated. History has a way of sneaking up on us. We don't usually head toward the great social changes in a straight line; we get there by taking lots of little turns along the way. The proliferation of fast food is just one response to most people's shrinking amount of personal time in an ever-more-pressured workplace. We start earlier, finish later, yet are still stretched to the limit to make ends meet. The age when a man was able to support his family on the wages from a forty-hour week is over. Now everyone has to pitch in and many homes are empty for ten to twelve hours each day. The family regroups in the early evening, too exhausted to cope with the idea of cooking and cleaning up a meal; so they buy takeout, which may or may not be eaten in the car. They no longer enjoy the daily communion around the dinner table or the satisfaction of giving and receiving the fruits of their work. They simply survive, trying to get enough rest between the household chores to face another day. So much for civilization . . .

The trouble is that we're not only robbing our children of one of the fulcrums of family life, but we may also be setting some potentially frightening trends for their future. In 1996, the powers-that-be gathered in Rome for a World Food Summit. This was no junket (they went in November, when the weather isn't good); it was a serious meeting of minds about how this planet's agriculture is going to keep up with its exploding population. At the present rate of growth, they say, we can expect to be welcoming an extra three billion souls into the world by the year 2030. This will pose a huge problem for our farmers, who will have to produce 75 percent more food, if one in ten of us aren't to starve. Since we're also running out of cultivable space, the solutions we come up with will have to be fairly radical, involving all sorts of decisions about complicated issues like water management, agroforestry, biodiversity, aquaculture, biointensive agriculture, and efficient energy use. At this point I glaze over because I simply don't know enough. But I do understand that many of the choices about how, where, and what is grown—in this country, at least—will depend on us.

We are the market and if we continue to demand (i.e. buy) a wide variety of fresh fruits, vegetables, spices, meats, fish, and cheeses, agribusiness will do its best to continue to supply us. But if our increasing dependence on fast food leads that demand to taper off, the companies will follow the profit and convert vast tracts of farmland for the growing of just one or two crops. Eventually, foods that are so familiar now would start to disappear, until they could be found only in specialty stores—where a carton of cow's milk might cost as much as caviar does today. The one question remaining to our children then will be "how do you want your soy?" They will ask it of their kids, who won't believe that burgers were once made of beef.

Personally, I prefer to argue with Charley about what we eat now than have to confess to her later that it was my carelessness—and that of millions like me—which cost her a whole wondrous way of life.

Keeping the Feast

HE WOMAN LOOKED EXHAUSTED, WEIGHED down by her armloads of brightly colored shopping bags. She slumped on to the seat next to me and slipped off her shoes, splaying out red toes on the cool marble floor. The air around us was full of the smell of synthetic cinnamon and the sounds of seasonal Muzak being piped through the mall. "Yeah"—she sneered to no one in particular—"jingle, jingle, jingle . . ." I smiled sympathetically, understanding exactly how she felt. I'm a veteran of many such Christmas campaigns, all waged with a view to recapturing that magic of childhood—all too busy and frantic to even come close.

I would often wonder how my mother did it. She was a working woman, too, yet always seemed to have the holidays under reasonable control. As a child, I knew that preparations had begun the night I came home from school to find our oak table polished to a deep gleam and pushed against the wall. Over the next few days Mom would fill it with a cornucopia of Christmas treats: tangy-sweet tangerines; a huge wooden bowl of walnuts; fresh dates and figs; crystallized fruits; and, my favorite, round boxes of Turkish Delight, dredged in confectioners' sugar. My hands would twitch every time I walked by, but I didn't dare touch; my mother would have smacked anyone who snuck so much as a peanut before we'd started the festival properly at church on Christmas Eve.

The scent of waxed wood would propel me down our long hallway to the kitchen at the back, where I knew Mum would be making her mince pies. She made her own mincemeat, too, and I'll never forget rounding the corner to be assaulted by that rich fragrance of fruit, fresh-baked pastry, and warm sugar. There was always a small plate of rejects waiting on the counter, and when their sweetness melted around my taste buds, the holidays had truly begun.

The excitement would continue to mount for a couple of weeks as Dad took me to see Father Christmas (as we called him) and the Oxford Street Lights, while Mum spent increasing hours slaving at the stove. Every now and then she'd let me help, showing me how to make her delicious trifle or spread the icing on her chocolate log. I don't remember much about the parties we were cooking for, but those afternoons with her are crystal clear. We talked, we laughed, she taught, I learned, we had fun. I felt closer to her then than at any other time, and when Nana Moyce joined us in the kitchen, it was as if a circle was complete. They were among the most golden moments of my Christmas, but I wouldn't truly appreciate them for many years to come.

As a young adult, I thought the success of this celebration depended simply on its trimmings. The more plentiful the food, the happier the occasion; the prettier the setting, the more comfortable we'd be. I shopped, decorated, and cooked for months, until my body and bank account almost broke under the strain. The menus I drew up were gargantuan; they read like Christmas dinner at a four-star hotel. In 1983, for instance, I made a total of twenty-two different recipes. The hors d'oeuvres were smoked-salmon soufflé, pâté de foie, and baby quiches. The appetizer was crab ramekins; followed by leek-and-Stilton soup; followed by roast rib of beef, Yorkshire pudding, roast potatoes, roast parsnips, braised brussels sprouts, glazed carrots, gravy, and horseradish sauce; followed by a cucumber sorbet to clear the palate; followed by a selection of cheeses with which to finish our wine; followed by Christmas pudding, with brandy butter and/or whipped cream; followed by an orange sorbet; followed by coffee served with mince pies, stuffed dates, chocolate-dipped cherries, and coconut ice. There was also a fruitcake on hand for those who might feel peckish later.

It was complete overkill, an exhausting effort that left me in no mood to see the guests I'd worked so hard to please. They came, anyway, and we spent a few uncomfortable hours together eating too much food, drinking too much wine, and indulging in the usual seasonal sparring across the Christmas table. By six o'clock that evening, it was over for another year and I was left to do the dishes, wondering what went wrong.

When I came to this country, things only got worse. Contrary to popular belief, our modern Christmas was not invented back in Britain, it was invented over here. America gave the world our present-day versions of Santa Claus, the Christmas card, and put a tannenbaum into every Christian home. She borrowed from each of her children's cultures, combining customs and recipes from all their motherlands, until she had created the complicated chaos we celebrate today. Here, I had to have cookies, candies, plum pudding; stollen bread, eggnog, mulled wine; inside decorations, outside decorations, an enormous tree; big gifts, stocking stuffers, small tokens of affection; cards, wrapping, ribbons, wreaths—the list went on and on. The holiday had turned into an endurance test, so I slapped the plastic down and spared myself the strain. At least, I did until Charley came along.

My daughter understands the spirit of the season better than almost anyone else I know. She likes her holiday traditions to have a story behind them and isn't interested in any treat or trimming that we can't make ourselves. She loves to hear about my Mum, whom she never met in life, as she slices the cherries to decorate the trifle; and when she stirs the Christmas pudding and makes her special wish, I'm required to repeat the tale of the silver sixpence that was once hidden for me in Nana Moyce's mix. Charley is my hope for the future and the keeper of my past. She makes me reach back to these much-loved women and the recipes they handed down, while at the same time making me think ahead to the day when she will pass them on in her turn. She reminds me that our time together is brief and much too precious to throw away on unnecessary worry. Who cares if our cookies are lopsided or the candies didn't set, as long as they were made at the blissfully messy baking session when her grandfather helped out? My dad's annual arrival at the airport is the official start to Charley's holiday, the point from which her family is together and she's surrounded by their love.

Her bright little face is the magic of Christmas. It shone into my darkest corners and showed me where to find the simplicity I'd lost. She doesn't need me to be slaving in the kitchen for a dozen different parties or stalking the mall in search of all those gifts. She needs me to be home with her, creating the memories together that we'll both cherish for a lifetime. Those golden moments when we talked, we laughed, I taught, she learned, and we made lots of Mum's mince pies.

Mincemeat Tart

This is a variation on those little pies of my mum's and makes a nice dessert for a Christmas buffet or potluck party. The mincemeat gets better and better with age, so the quantities below allow for half the jars to be put away until next Christmas!

The mincemeat

6 cups finely grated beef suet

3 cups golden raisins

6 large pears—
    peeled and chopped

3 cups blanched, sliced almonds

3 cups raisins

6 large apples—peeled and
    chopped

2 cups mixed peel

thin peel of 2 oranges and
    2 lemons

Wash and chop the above and mix well together. Then add the following:

3 cups currants

juice from the oranges
    and lemons

¼ teaspoon ginger

1½ pounds brown sugar

½ pint sherry

2 cups chopped dried apricots

½ fresh nutmeg, finely grated

½ teaspoon each ground cloves
    and cinnamon

1 pint brandy

1 cup maple syrup

1. Mix all the ingredients together and put in a large saucepan and warm through. 2. Put into clean, warm jars and process in a boiling-water bath for 10 minutes.

To make the crust

　¼ cup shortening　　　　　¾ cup flour
　½ teaspoon salt　　　　　 2 tablespoons chilled water

1. Mix the shortening with the flour and salt. 2. Draw together with about 2 tablespoons of chilled water. 3. Roll into a ball and chill the pastry for 1 hour. 4. Roll it out and line a tart tin.

The topping

　1 cup flour　　　　　　　½ cup brown sugar
　½ cup butter　　　　　　 1 teaspoon cinnamon
　1 teaspoon vanilla　　　　⅓ cup chopped hazelnuts

1. Combine all the dry ingredients 2. Cut the butter into the mix. 3. Rub the butter in with the fingertips until it is crumbly.

To finish the tart

1. Make up 1/2 cup of the topping. 2. Bake the tart crust for about 20 minutes. 3. Fill the tart with mincemeat. 4. Sprinkle with topping and bake the tart for about 20 minutes until the topping is golden brown. 5. Serve warm or cold with whipped cream on the side.

Plum Pudding

As a child, I used to love waiting for the entrance of the pudding at the end of our Christmas meal. The lights would be put out and my mother would bring in this ball of flickering blue flame, which everyone would applaud. When the lights were put back on, I would poke about my plate looking for the sixpenny-bit that my grandmother always hid in the mix. I never ate a mouthful, because to me, "Christmas pud" tasted like boiled tires. Today, I have revised my opinion and our feast wouldn't be complete without this dark, moist dessert, slathered in brandy sauce.

1½ cups finely grated suet
8 cups fresh breadcrumbs
1 cup raisins
1 cup candied peel
1 lemon
1¼ cups fine sugar
1 teaspoon cinnamon
½ teaspoon cloves
⅔ cup brandy
3½ cups flour

¾ cup currants
1 cup golden raisins
4 large apples—peeled and
  chopped
1 orange
1½ cups brown sugar
1 teaspoon nutmeg
4 eggs
1 cup dark beer

1. Grate the rinds of the orange and lemon, and extract their juice. 2. Peel, core, and chop the apples. 3. Mix the fruit, nuts, peel, and citrus rinds together in a large bowl. 4. Stir in the flour, spices, breadcrumbs, sugar, and suet. 5. Beat the eggs, then add the brandy and juices. 6. Fold into the flour-and-fruit mixture. 7. Mix in enough beer to bring the pudding to a dropping consistency. (Let everyone stir the pudding at this point. It is an old English tradition and they each get to make a special Christmas wish!) 8. Cover the bowl and leave overnight. 9. In the morning, mix again and pour into buttered pudding bowls. 10. Wrap the bowls in muslin and secure with string. 11. Place a small bowl upside down in a large pan and stand the pudding on this. 12. Pour in enough boiling water to come halfway up the bowl. Keep the water at this level throughout cooking. 13. Cover the pan and steam the pudding for 8–9 hours, checking the water level frequently. (If you wish, this can be made days in advance. Cook the pudding for 5 or 6 hours, allow it to cool, then store in a cool place. Complete the steaming on Christmas Day.) 14. Before serving, warm 1/2 cup of brandy in a pan. 15. Decorate the pudding with a sprig of holly and pour the warmed brandy over it. Set light to it as you enter the dining room. 16. Serve with brandy sauce (see below) or whipped cream on the side.

Brandy Sauce

1 cup heavy cream	1 cup milk
½ cup brandy	3 eggs
3 tablespoons brown sugar	freshly grated nutmeg

1. Mix the milk and cream together and warm in a bowl over boiling water. 2. Separate the eggs and beat the yolks with the sugar. 3. Beat into warming milk, a little at a time. 4. Cook until the sauce thickens, then remove from the heat and stir in the brandy. 5. Whip the egg whites until stiff and beat into the sauce. 6. Grate a little nutmeg over it before serving.

English Trifle

I include this recipe here because it is such a part of my family's Christmas, but really it's a dessert that can be made anytime and looks marvelous on a buffet table.

stale sponge cake	2 large bananas
6 eggs plus 1 yolk	2 pints milk

1 teaspoon vanilla
⅔ cup strawberry jam
whipped cream
slivered almonds
1 cup diced fresh pineapple

½ cup sugar
1 pack strawberry Jell-O
glacé cherries
slices of banana

1. Line a trifle bowl—or bowl of similar size—with pieces of stale cake. 2. Warm the jam in a pan until liquid and pour it over the cake. 3. Allow the jam to set. 4. Meanwhile make up the Jell-O with boiling water. 5. When the Jell-O is fully dissolved and a little cooler, stir in the diced pineapple. 6. Pour the Jell-O over the layer of jam and leave it to set in the refrigerator overnight. 7. In the morning, make a custard by beating the eggs and yolk with the sugar until pale and fluffy. 8. Warm the milk and vanilla together until just boiling. 9. Beat the milk into the eggs, a little at a time. 10. Slice the 2 bananas and stir into the custard. 11. Pour the custard over the layer of Jell-O. 12. Return the trifle to the refrigerator for the custard to set. 13. When the custard is firm, decorate the trifle with whipped cream, banana slices, glacé cherries, and a sprinkling of slivered almonds.

The Zen of Food

E HAD A COMPLICATED RELATIONSHIP, BUT then he was a complex character. He could change like the wind from cantankerous, to irate, to contemptuous, to apologetic, to affectionate, and finally into a real clown. There were times when I was so angry with him I could barely speak, then he'd blow gently into my face and my heart would melt. I should mention that I'm talking about Hotshot, our horse—an elderly strawberry roan we saved from the soap factory, several years ago.

I used to love watching him eat an apple. He did it with such grace and dedication. First, he'd look at it, then he'd smell it, then he'd extend his velvet lips, take it gently from my hand and drop it on the ground in front of him. Finally, he'd bite it neatly in two and start chewing the first half. At that point he retreated into apple bliss: his whole being concentrated on the task at hand. You could see it in his eyes: there was no taste, smell, sight, or sound other than that fruit. I could wave a whole bucket of grain in front of him and he wouldn't even notice until the apple was all gone.

We can learn a lot from animals. They live entirely in the moment, instinct telling them that this might be the only one. When Hotshot drank water from the pond, he did it so intently that you could almost feel the cool gush flowing down his throat, but he was no less serious when he lifted his head to sniff the morning breeze or took off at a gallop across his field. His behavior was a far cry from us humans, who seem to revel in doing lots of things at once.

Take eating, as an example. How often do we sit at a table and eat a meal in silence? Come to that, how often do we sit at table to eat a meal at all? Don't most of us these days find ourselves nibbling standing up, or while we're on the phone, or as we're watching the TV? The other night I caught myself doing all three simultaneously; no wonder I sometimes suffer from acid indigestion. . . . Tables now seem to be reserved for formal meals, usually when we're entertaining. Even then, our attention is diverted from our food as we take care of our guests or get lost in conversation. The question is, with all these distractions, do we ever truly taste whatever it is we're eating—and exactly how do we know when we're really full?

Recently, I spent a day conducting an experiment: eating food the Hotshot way. I began with my early-morning coffee, which I took outside to drink quietly on the porch. First, I looked into its dark depths and thought of all the human effort—the planting, the tending, the picking, the roasting, the blending—that had gone into that one cup. Then I closed my eyes and breathed in its aroma, letting its fragrance fill my nose. I took a sip and held it, to give my taste buds a chance before I swallowed. Finally I let it go, trying to follow it as it hit the back of my throat. The difference was amazing! That drink had flavors that I'd never noticed before. It smelled like hazelnuts, but tasted more of dark chocolate, and I only got the coffee part on the back half of my tongue. I tried the same procedure with the rest of it and found, when I had finished, that I didn't want my customary second cup at all.

The day was full of such revelations. By sitting still and eating in silence, I could concentrate on all the sensations of my food. At lunch, I discovered that just one slice of my beloved salami was actually so salty that it needed to be counterbalanced with a whole plate of fruit. While at dinner, the boiled rice which I normally disdain turned out to be the most surprising item on the menu. Some mouthfuls tasted buttery, some tasted nutty, while others had little flashes of scented or spicy flavor from the parsley-and-black-pepper seasonings. Greg seemed disappointed when I sat back, leaving my plate half-full. "Didn't you like it?" he asked anxiously. "I loved it!" I assured him. "I've just had enough. I'm sated. You know—satisfied, replete. From now on, a half-empty plate is the biggest compliment I can pay you." He looked unconvinced, but I have noticed since my experiment that when I'm paying attention to my meal, I enjoy it more thoroughly in much smaller portions.

I wish I could thank Hotshot for this new insight with a large, luscious Granny Smith—but he passed away the other day. It was nothing dramatic; he was very old and his body just gave out. I hope that there's a horse heaven for him to go to, a place where he'll know that he taught his human how to appreciate her food . . . a place where they have apples.

The Digestif

ND SO WE'VE COME TO THE END OF OUR GATH-
ering and it's time to write the thank-you notes.
This has been the best kind of book to work on because it has taught me something, too, and I'll never treat my
food casually again. I would especially like to thank my editor,
Susan Allison, for inviting me to the table in the first place and
for being such a patient and encouraging companion along the
way.

Deep debts of gratitude are also owed to my father, Michael
Jacobson, who so expertly put the icing on the cake; to the won-

derful Jacque Schultze, for finding so many of the essential ingredients; and to my dear friend and agent, Regula Noetzli, for her unwavering faith. And I mustn't forget Steve Kowalski, Deborah Huchison, Jim Hawkins, Jonathan Hess, and Kathy Strahm, who all sampled my ideas with such enthusiasm; or the ladies of the Brown County Library: Yvonne Oliger, Mary Seibert, and Zoe Kean, who gave me so much help.

Finally, my love and thanks must go to Greg and Charley for keeping the spice in my life throughout this project. Now it's my turn to entertain you and—yes, Greg—it's time for sushi.